Local Space
Relocation Astrology

By
Michael Erlewine

The Astrology of Local Space

An ebook from

Startypes.com
315 Marion Avenue
Big Rapids, Michigan 49307

First published 2007

© 2006 Michael Erlewine / StarTypes.com

ISBN 978-0-9798328-3-3

Graphic designs by Michael Erlewine

Some image elements © 2007 JupiterImages Corp.
Some image elements © IStockPhoto.com.

The Astrology of Local Space

This book is dedicated to

Russell Gregory

*Who lives in the lineage of
the Transcendentalists*

The Astrology of Local Space

The Astrology of Local Space

The Astrology of Local Space

The Astrology of Local Space

The Astrology of Local Space

The Astrology of Local Space

The Astrology of Local Space

Y

Local Space

I discovered Local Space astrology in the early 1970s and popularized it through a series of articles over the next few years. More than anything else, I programmed this technique and made Local Space available to astrologers all over the world. Today it is part of most major astrological software packages and is considered one of the main relocation techniques in modern astrology. Indeed it is a wonderful technique.

I have included two of my original articles on Local Space later in this text. You may want to read that first article, "The Astrology of Local Space" to catch my words when they were brand new.

The Astrology of Local Space

Y

"There! Where Power hovers"

Here is a brief quote from that original article:

"Here is no "subtle plane," but a personal landscape painted in bold and clear strokes and tailor made to fit the psyche of each individual. Here is a world where the modern man is learning to move across the face of this earth in an endless dance of adjustment and tuning of his radix -- of his self. Individuals driven in particular directions on a checkerboard world, unable to resist travelling toward a goal that is no particular place on earth so much as it is a direction imprinted within them, the direction of a force or planet, "There! Where Power hovers", to use Don Juan's expression.

11

The Astrology of Local Space

In a word, here is perhaps the must vulgar astrological system, where the obvious is enthroned and the subtle unnecessary."

YYY

The Pull of a Force Drawing us Closer

As the above quote suggests, relocation and the endless day-to-day adjustments of our living quarters that go with it may not just be the obvious move to another house or another city as much as it is a need to fulfill something deep within us, the pull of a planet, the pull of a force drawing us closer, an inner need and desire to know that force better and to experience it.

The Astrology of Local Space

A Day or Part of a Day

Getting away on a vacation and having that unexpected rush of freedom and delight as we move for a day or part of a day into almost another world, a world we feel free to experience, as we soak in an undefined quality that we just can't seem to get enough of. Later, heading home almost in a swoon, some little part of our heart is just too tender to touch, as we reluctantly leave the place.

Places do have power and Local Space is a study of the power of places over us and how to choose places that will fulfill us. I hope you enjoy exploring Local Space astrology.

The Astrology of Local Space

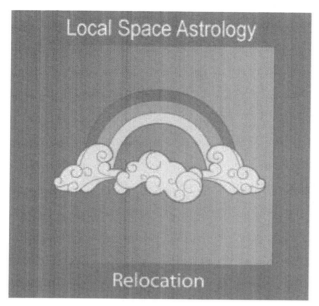

Where Should I Live?

As a counseling astrologer with some 40 years of experience, perhaps the most frequent question this astrologer is asked (aside from relationship and marriage analysis) in a counseling session is: "Where is a good place for me to live?"

Of course the answer to that question depends on a number factors, and it often involves one of several astrological relocation techniques.

That there are better and worse locations for each of us there can be little doubt. Most of us know this from our own life experience. We feel differently in different locations. Our winter vacation in Acapulco may have

The Astrology of Local Space

been glorious or an experience we hope to never repeat. That is the power of places.

Saving Time with Relocation

And relocation, moving yourself and your family to a new home, perhaps even in a new city or a different part of the world is familiar to many of us. But there is another aspect of relocation astrology that is perhaps not so well understood, and that is that we can achieve instantly by relocation what otherwise might only be achieved over a long period of time. Let me explain.

Those of us who have studied astrology know that there are events waiting out there in our future that

The Astrology of Local Space

will affect us for better or for worse. Professional astrologers use astrological techniques like transits and progressions to pinpoint future events that will impact each of us personally. An example of this might perhaps be a major Saturn transit or bringing the progressed Sun to a conjunction with our natal Venus. These are coming events that are astrologically significant and that even now cast their shadows on our present life. They are out there waiting until their time. Let's take a hypothetical example:

The Astrology of Local Space

Planet Chakras   Venus

Venus or compassion is the key to life here on Earth, and has always been so.

Progression in Space

Suppose we are looking forward to a Venus event, something that will activate our sense of love, compassion, or our ability to feel and appraise things. Perhaps these qualities are absent in our life or of such minor magnitude that we know we need more of whatever they represent. Astrologically, we can look at our transits and/or progressions, scanning the future with astrological techniques for Venus events that in time will impact us.

However, using relocation techniques, we can see that by moving to a particular city we can bring about a Venus experience at once, just by relocating to that

The Astrology of Local Space

location. And if we aren't able to relocate, we can at least travel there on vacation and bathe in whatever experience that location may provide.

In other words, we can achieve by a relocation in space what otherwise we might have to wait in time for to have the same experience. It is this ability to more-or-less instantly gratify a deep inner need that makes relocation astrology so popular today. We don't have to wait five or fifty years for an auspicious transit or progressed aspect. Instead, we can examine our relocation possibilities and act on them whenever we like.

Perhaps best of all we can take a one-day trip or a longer vacation at various auspicious locations and get some sense of whether we like it there. We can see what happens to us in that locale, whether it is fun and an enhancement or no-fun, disappointing.

The Astrology of Local Space

The Various Types of Relocation Techniques

While there are many relocation techniques that have been used in astrology, but three stand out as the most popular today. They are:

(1) Relocated Angles and Houses

(2) Astro-Geography

(3) Local Space Astrology

Perhaps the oldest of the three methods (Relocated Angles and Houses) involves relocating the natal chart angles and houses, which is as simple as casting a chart for your birth day and time, but for another locality – a different place. Once this is done,

The Astrology of Local Space

you compare house placement in the relocation chart with the natal chart.

The second relocation type, "Astro-Geography" is a method (using a standard geographic map) to draw lines where the various heavenly bodies are on one of the four angles, Ascendant, Descendant, Midheaven, and Imum Coeli (IC). Both of these methods are explained in more detail at the end of this book.

And last but not least, there is Local Space astrology, which is the main topic of this book. I must admit I am partial to Local Space astrology, having invented the technique myself, back in the early 1970s. Today it is included in most major astrological software, although I am no longer always sited as its founder. Ah well.

The Astrology of Local Space

Local Space Astrology

The beauty of Local Space astrology is its simplicity. Just imagine that at your birth, your mother picked you up in her arms and walked outside. As she sat in the soft evening light of summer with you in her arms, she could see the Moon rising in the East, the very last rays of the Sun setting in the West, and Jupiter and Venus shining brightly in the twilight. This is what Local Space is all about, the directions of planets and the directions of cities as they appear from your birthplace.

The Astrology of Local Space

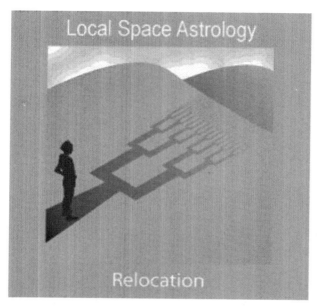

Stars on Earth

The Sun, Moon, Venus, and Jupiter (and all the other non-visible) planets are not only directions in the sky, but they are directions also here on Earth. In other words, a planet like Venus hovering low on the horizon, let's say in the southeast, passes not only through whatever zodiac constellation it happens to be in, but also through any number of cities on the surface of the earth. A line or direction in heaven is simultaneously a line and direction down here on earth.

The Astrology of Local Space

Heavens on Earth

This is what Local Space is all about, noting that the lines that the planets trace in the heavens are also lines traced down here on earth, lines that run across the earth, passing through any number of cities and places. In Local Space, we want to know which cities can be found along the line for each planet.

For example, we each have a Venus line that runs all around the earth, the line and direction Venus was in at our birth. Whatever we might agree that Venus represents in astrology (things like love, care, appraisal, compassion, etc.) are accented for us

23

The Astrology of Local Space

along our particular Venus line as it appeared at our birth.

Traveling, relocating, or even receiving a letter, phone call, or email from that direction, will activate Venus for us to some degree. Whether that will be a good or bad experience for us is something we each must find out for ourselves.

The Astrology of Local Space

Article I: Local Space Astrology

[Editor's Note: The following article was first published in 1977 in the 6th number of the "Cosmecology Bulletin" as published by Charles A. Jayne. Although astrologers had worked with the Horizon system before, Erlewine was the first to define the concept of local space as presented here. In particular, the combining of Celestial positions (stars, planets, etc.) with directions on the globe (cities, places, etc.) and the concept of relocating toward a planet first appeared in this publication. This was before the advent of the home computer and Erlewine had worked out the tedious mathematics of local space first on a simple calculator and later on one of the programmables.]

The Astrology of Local Space

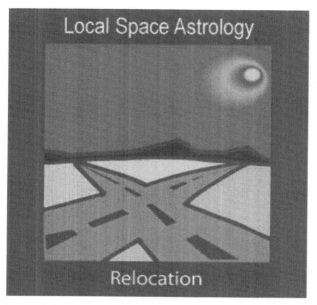

Local Space Astrology

I want to relate to you a powerful new way (new to me) of coming to know yourself through astrology. It involves another kind of map or chart of our birth moment, a map of the actual space surrounding the birthplace, and this form of topo-centric astrology I call the astrology of "Local Space." First I should tell you how I happened on to this fascinating approach.

I was involved in an attempt at understanding the many different house systems that astrologers use, trying to decide which of all of them might be the best for my own purposes. For several years I had not used any house system at all, using instead only the

The Astrology of Local Space

four angles of the chart in a kind of protest or disgust at the lack of agreement among astrologers concerning systems of house division. It seemed rather strange to me that there were so many competing house systems.

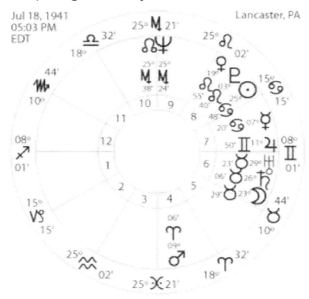

Astrological House Systems

For many of the years in my astrological practice I lacked the necessary mathematical background to decide for myself which of the many house systems made sense to me. I could only read about the merits of each house system and take the word of those who supposedly knew. I came to use the Campanus system of houses because some of those astrologers

The Astrology of Local Space

that I respected most (Charles A. Jayne, for example) used this system. In recent years, I had been learning enough spherical trigonometry on my pocket calculator to be able to make my first attempt at solving the mystery of house division for myself.

I have always been a slow learner when it comes to mathematics, so I had to sit down with an equatorial star-map of the constellations and attempt to draw out graphically the various ways of dividing space and time, in hope of being enlightened as to which house system had the most going for it. Of course, I wanted to draw out the house systems using my own natal chart. This was kind of complex, for I had to calculate (using spherical trigonometry) the 360 degrees of my natal horizon and plot this curving line on the star-map.

The Astrology of Local Space

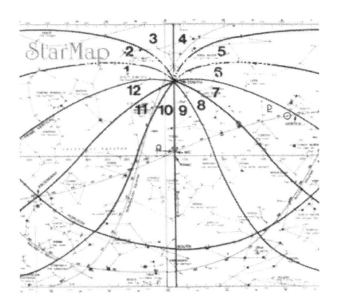

House Systems Drawn Out

All house systems agree on the validity of the horizon, so I felt this was the place to start. This proved to be a most worthwhile exercise. I soon became aware that regardless of which house system was used, what was of interest to most astrologers was not the entire 360-degrees of the horizon, but just those few places where it crossed or intersected the familiar zodiac or ecliptic, places like the Ascendant and Midheaven, for example.

In other words, house systems in general are concerned with different ways of sending meaningful lines to intersect the zodiac, and these intersecting

29

The Astrology of Local Space

points are then the cusps or sensitive points for that individual, a kind of astrologer's acupuncture points.

Laying these different house systems out graphically on a map helped a great deal to understand what in fact the various house systems were, but I yearned for some simpler way to deal with it all. I reached a point where I took the problem into my own hands and said, "O.K. Michael, let's suspend judgment on which of all these house systems is best for you and do something very simple, that although perhaps unsophisticated, will make sense to you."

The Astrology of Local Space

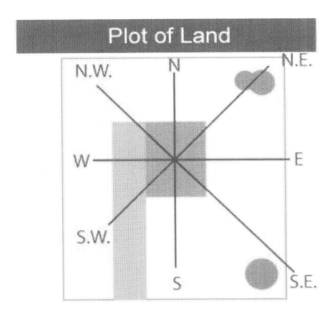

Plot of Land

Local Space at Birthplace

I started off by making the center of the house system the place where one is born and I put the pole of the system overhead the pole of the birthplace, a point that is called the Zenith. Instead of using more complex methods of division, I just divided the space surround my birth into a simple pie of twelve equal divisions radiating out from the birthplace. This represented on the earth (geographically) and thru space (astronomically). This, then, would be my very own house system! The points where the twelve radiating lines intersected the zodiac plane would be the house cusps or sensitive points in this system.

The Astrology of Local Space

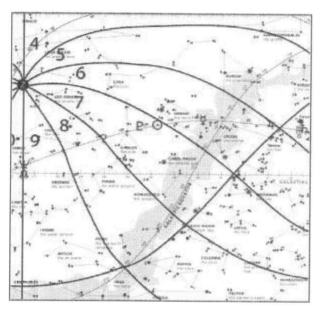

Radiant House System

I was, at this point no different from the other astrologers who had developed their own house systems. I did find that, although this method of house division was quite radical compared to the more familiar systems, the particular cusp degrees of the zodiac had already proved significant and were already "favorite" and previously noted points along my zodiac. I had, in my own way, stumbled upon what I found out was already known as the Horizontal House system, which, along with the Campanus system, represents one of two obvious and complementary ways to divide the space surrounding a birth into equal parts. I named my version the

The Astrology of Local Space

"Radiant House System," because it consisted of radiating lines from the birth place, and I like the play on the word "radiance."

The Merry-Go-Round

The astrologer L. Edward Johndro calls the Campanus System "the ferris wheel", and the Radiant or Horizontal System "the merry-go-round." Astrologer Charles A. Jayne had been pointing out the need to investigate this Horizontal system of houses for many years. At that point, I was still interested in those twelve little points where the radiating house lines intersected the old familiar zodiac, the so-called "cusps."

The Astrology of Local Space

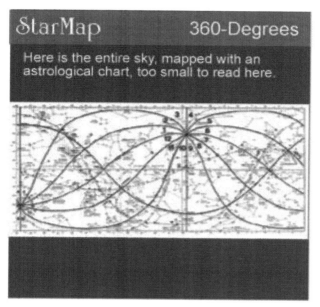

StarMap — 360-Degrees

Here is the entire sky, mapped with an astrological chart, too small to read here.

The 360-Degrees of the Horizon

Then something very important began to occur to me. I began to see that the horizon itself was more than just 12 house cusps. It was a complete circle in itself, just as the zodiac is, stretching a full 360 degrees around the heavens. Instead of considering the horizon as a necessary means to get at and define these zodiacal pressure points, the cusps, I began to follow on the star-map the line of my radix horizon thru the heavens to the point where it intersected the plane or line of the zodiac on this map. This point was, of course, my ascendant at about 8-degrees of Sagittarius. But my eyes kept going past the ascendant, following my natal horizon until it

The Astrology of Local Space

intersected another line: that of the plane of our galaxy, at which point the first shock rolled in. My horizon intersected the galactic plane in the constellation Cygnus (the swan).

Cygnus the Swan

At this point, I have to relate a somewhat more personal story to make clear what was happening. Over the past years, I had been assembling a book called "Astrophysical Directions" containing stellar points and planes, and in the process I had to calculate and plot quite a few maps of the heavens. In this way, I came to know and develop a sense of the

The Astrology of Local Space

major constellations in a much more intimate way than I had before.

Throughout this work, I noted a "fixation" on a couple of constellations in particular. Above them all, I had a special reverence for the constellation Cygnus. Who knows why? On repeated occasions (for no reason I could determine) I had felt such deep identification with this constellation and what it seemed to signify that tears came to my eyes.

The Astrology of Local Space

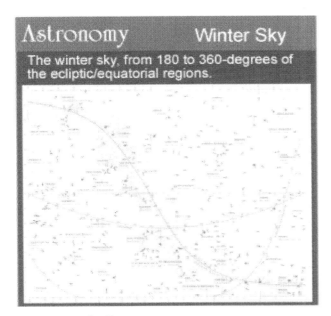

Astronomy   Winter Sky

The winter sky, from 180 to 360-degrees of the ecliptic/equatorial regions.

Vela, the Sails

Now I find that Cygnus was one of the two constellations where my own particular horizon crossed the great plane of our galaxy -- a kind of galactic descendant and ascendant, the other being the constellation Vela, the sails -- also a constellation to which I have always been very sensitive.

Well, at this point I had to laugh. What, I said to myself, if the entire 360 degrees of the horizon of my birth is as sensitive as the node where it crosses the zodiac (Ascendant), did I have a galactic and supergalactic ascendant and new sets of constellations or "signs" to come to know?

The Astrology of Local Space

Here, I will shrink a long and (to me of course) beautiful story and just say that this discovery was the first of a great many such mini-enlightenments I was to have as my awareness grew beyond the limits of traditional zodiac. Over the next few months, I traced myself thru these star fields in some kind of personal odyssey and came to understand much more concerning my particular orientation or "attitude" toward the cosmos: first and not least, that I had one at all!

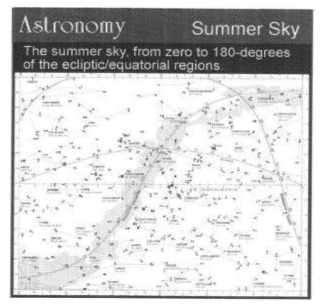

Astronomy　　Summer Sky

The summer sky, from zero to 180-degrees of the ecliptic/equatorial regions.

The Power of the Horizon

And I searched through my collection of horoscopes to see how my friends and acquaintances were oriented. I was discovering the strength and power of the local horizon. I had accepted and used the Ascendant, Vertex, and other sensitive ecliptic points in my work, but always with the accent on the zodiac. It had never occurred to me that in each case it took another plane to bring these nodes or points of intersection into existence -- in this case, it was the plane of the horizon.

And yet I had, in a subconscious way, used the horizon in all my work. I could now see that each individual has a kind of unique orientation or attitude to the whole cosmos and that in the horizon we have a power plane capable of revealing much more about our self than just those twelve sensitive points which relate to the familiar zodiac.

The Astrology of Local Space

Astronomy — Summer Sky

The summer sky, from 0 to 180-degrees of the ecliptic/equatorial regions.

Exploring the Heavens

At any rate, I began to explore the whole of the heavens from my personal point of view. And, for a time, I forgot the zodiac and instead began to inquire into these other planes and thus came to learn a great deal that was new about my own attitude and orientation to my birth event, to my life.

The Astrology of Local Space

Local Space Astrology

Relocation

What about Geographic Maps?

Somewhere during this time, another idea occurred to me that proved to be most compelling: of course the horizon also traced a path on maps of the earth, as well as the heavens. I had calculated, by this time, a complete chart of the planets positions in the horizon system using the system's equivalent to zodiac longitude and latitude, which astronomer's call azimuth and altitude. How, I wondered, would the directions of the planets in my horizon chart relate to directions and cities on this earth? A door opened.

I soon developed the trigonometry needed to answer these questions -- quite a prodigious undertaking for

The Astrology of Local Space

me and thus began a real magical mystery tour through my life history. Although I have lived in several different places, the one major move in my lifetime up to that point had been from Lancaster, Pennsylvania (my birthplace) to Ann Arbor, Michigan. Of course what I wanted to know was: in what direction was Ann Arbor from Lancaster? That is, what degree and direction did Ann Arbor occupy on my radix or birth horizon?

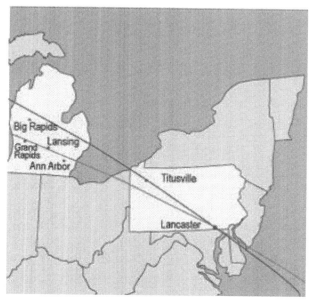

Ann Arbor is My Jupiter

And here rolled in the second great shock wave. It turns out that Ann Arbor is right in the direction of my natal Jupiter position on the local space chart -- within

The Astrology of Local Space

2 degrees. In other words, a move to Ann Arbor was a move in the direction of my natal Jupiter. Jupiter rules my Ascendant and its position above the 7th house cusp had made it very prominent in any analysis of my chart.

I wondered at such a coincidence and set out to answer some of the other questions that now began popping up in my mind. What about the other places I had lived or to which I had traveled or thought of travelling to? The history of my travel came before my mind... some places of joy and learning, others of sorrow and pain. I plotted the directions and calculated the charts for all of these places and what I found through reading these charts was overwhelming. It marked my initial surrender to what now appears to be, for me, a major discovery in my personal astrological life, that of an astrology of local space.

The Astrology of Local Space

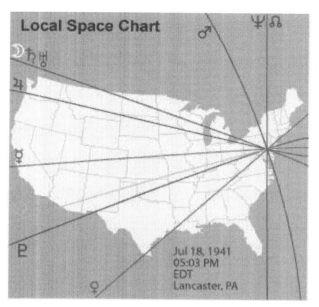

Local Space Chart

Jul 18, 1941
05:03 PM
EDT
Lancaster, PA

Local Space Lines

I erected different local space charts. These amounted to maps of the space surrounding each place as if I had been born there, rather than at Lancaster. The story of my life and 'self', interpreted and confirmed through my reading of these local space charts was, in a word, moving.

Let me cite an example of the sort of thing I found. I am well known to my friends as being a homebody. It is very difficult for anything to induce me to leave my home. Yet, at one point in my life, however, I sold everything I owned. My wife and I moved north to go into the green plant business, to manage our own

The Astrology of Local Space

greenhouses. I actually left Ann Arbor and moved away! As it so happened, we were a couple of years ahead of our time in offering fine, green-house plants to people; the demand for these plants and the plant store craze did not appear until later in time. We lost everything in this venture. On the material or investment plane, it was a complete disaster.

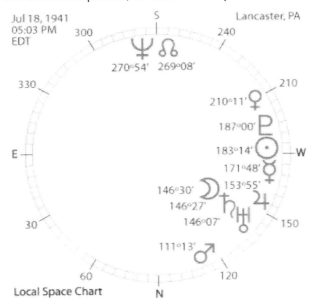

Local Space Chart

Triple Conjunction

Now, in my local space chart I have triple conjunction of the Moon, Uranus, and Saturn and to the same degree, all three bodies conjunct within less than half a degree. In anybody's astrology, this would be accounted quite a strong focus. The move into the

45

The Astrology of Local Space

greenhouse business was a move precisely -- to the degree -- into (or toward) this triple conjunction! I had actually moved into my Moon/Uranus/Saturn conjunction! It was as if we had gone there to wrestle and come to terms with my Saturn (or with Satan, you might say) -- and we came out the wiser for it.

For this experience, as hard as it was, ended many more superficial fears on my part concerning loss. We lost what to us at that time was everything, and still our life went on. And so I could go on, telling the story of my life as confirmed through local space charts. I won't though, but will pass from a personal account to a summary of what I have found through research into local space charts since my initial discovery.

The Astrology of Local Space

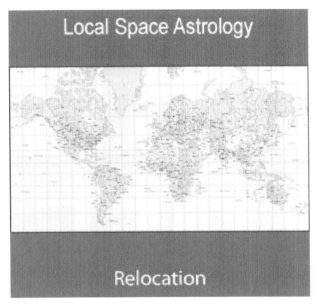

Voyage of Discovery

What had impressed me thru this voyage of discovery was the potency of the entire horizon as opposed to just a couple of its points (ascendant, vertex), and that somehow the orientation of an individual to the cosmos made a difference -- or was reflected in behavior and activity at the super-mundane level. It took me quite a while to develop the faith or let myself believe that 'God' or the spirit in us was so thorough in influence as to be all-pervading down to the finest details. Yet my spiritual teacher had some years before endlessly told me, "Michael, my God is no

The Astrology of Local Space

beggar. I don't have to make the ends meet. The ends already meet!"

Heaven on Earth

It was a while more before I could entertain with grace the idea that this same orientation or attitude was reflected as much upon the map of the earth as upon the map of the heavens. Another way of putting this (and this is, to me, the beauty of local space astrology), is that Heaven and Earth are interchangeable -- or are in the last analysis, one living entity -- a single whole. As my teacher would say, "This is it!"

The Astrology of Local Space

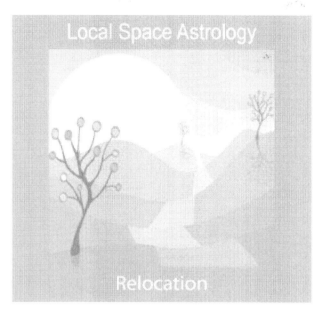

Almost Psychedelic

Celestial and Mundane

With the local space chart, this was made ever so
clear, a chart where every object in the universe,
celestial and mundane, has an equal and valid
position. Not only the planets and the stars, but on an
equal basis cities, countries, and even the local water
tower or friends' houses can be represented. All that
concerns us is the direction in space, the orientation,
not the distance. In local space the heavens and
earth, the celestial and mundane (or geographic)
spheres, exist side by side and are interchangeable.
A star is a city is a neighbor. We can walk towards,

The Astrology of Local Space

write letters to, or get up and travel into, for instance, our seventh house: and what is perhaps more important, we do all the time!

The World of Don Juan

More startling yet, we can travel into our natal planets since they also represent a direction on the globe in the chart of local space. Here, in a hopeless intermingling of the various planes of reference and of objects, a strange, and I must confess, somewhat magical view of our world begins to unfold and emerge: one in which every city and friend becomes a radiating center of influence.

The Astrology of Local Space

In this sphere, the long tradition of witchcraft and magic begins to become understandable; here local deities and preferred directions become the rule and the world seems a tangle of significance. The psychedelic character in local space charts is unmistakable and appears to be intrinsic to the system. The world appears as kind of a grand talisman or vast ritual ground, and the closest popular image of a similar nature in modern consciousness is the remarkable world of Don Juan as generated by the author Carlos Castaneda.

The Astrology of Local Space

A Checkerboard World

Here is no "subtle plane", but a personal landscape painted in bold and clear strokes and tailor made to fit the psyche of each individual. Here is a world where the modern man is learning to move across the face of this earth in an endless dance of adjustment and tuning of his radix -- of his self. Individuals driven in particular directions on a checkerboard world, unable to resist travelling toward a goal that is no particular place on earth so much as it is a direction imprinted within them, the direction of a force or planet, "There! where Power hovers", to use Don Juan's expression. In a word, here is perhaps the must vulgar astrological system, where the obvious is enthroned and the subtle unnecessary.

The Astrology of Local Space

The Basics

Let me go over some of the basics again. In simple terms the local space chart is a map of the 360 degrees of the horizon surrounding an event such as birth, with the various planets' positions plotted on it. The map represents the full circle or plane of the horizon, rather than only the two points at which it intersects the ecliptic (known to astrologers as the ascendant & descendant). The wheel of this chart then describes the horizon of a place, much as turning around on one spot we might look toward the East, South, West, and North – full circle.

The Astrology of Local Space

The Plane of the Horizon

In this coordinate system, the fundamental plane to which all else is referred is, then, the horizon of the observer, and the positions of the various planets as they appear from this location are projected onto the horizon using the coordinates, azimuth and altitude. Azimuth is this system's equivalent of the zodiac longitude and is measured, for our purposes, from the East direction, thru the North and on around in a counter-clockwise direction -- in the same way that we measure the traditional signs and houses. Altitude, analogous to ecliptic latitude, is measured above and below the horizon to the poles from 0 to 90 degrees.

The Astrology of Local Space

Local Space Astrology

Relocation

Locality Shifts

The single most important use of local space in the astrologer/client relationship, in my experience, has been in locality shifts. "Where would be a good place for me to live?" is one of the more frequent questions asked this astrologer during a reading. In the past I have made use of the quite valid and useful traditional technique of adjusting the RAMC of the radix to the new locality and coming up with a new Ascendant, and so forth. The radix positions then are read in terms of these new angles. Local space is by nature suited to express both celestial and geographic positions on one map or chart. Its special nature

The Astrology of Local Space

introduces several concepts not encountered in other techniques. Let us take a look at some of these.

Map of Local Space

As I mentioned before, one can also plot the positions of cities and places on the earth on the map of the local space, so our next project then will be to translate all the important cities in our lives into their equivalent positions on the radix local space chart.

We should be sure to include not only the places we ourselves have lived or visited, but also the cities that we have always thought we might like to visit -- that bring a warm feeling to mind, and so forth. The positions of cities where friends and not-so-friendlies

The Astrology of Local Space

live, where there are business relationships, etc. should also be included. We then examine these places in terms of their positions (or directions) on the local space chart with these thoughts in mind: Are these cities in aspect, in particular by conjunction or opposition? Are they in alignment with planets in the chart? In what quadrants and houses do these cities fall, and are any on the angles?

Moving into the Direction of a Planet

I have found that individuals tend to move toward cities that are also in the direction of planets that represent the particular kind of energy they may require at that time. An individual, for instance,

The Astrology of Local Space

needing to invoke the key to success, often obtained through Jupiter, may make one or several moves in that direction. Although this concept is so simple as to almost be embarrassing, this technique has shown itself to be of great value. In any case, its value seems to be substantial rather than hypothetical.

Individuals and Places

The local space chart can show a concrete, measurable relationship for the individual to any place -- a relationship which can vary from individual to individual (even in the same locality) as much as their local space charts vary from one another.

The Astrology of Local Space

Whatever may be the intrinsic character of a place
(and places undoubtedly have this), a selection of
people could react very differently to it from the point
of view of each one's own make-up, moreover, each
could react differently at different times, under
different astrological directions, and coming to it from
different places or geographical directions. Although
the mathematics involved in this system may seem a
bit complex, the application of its technique is simple
and direct, and this does much to recommend it.

Relocated Local Space Charts

After the basic information in the radix local space
chart has been taken in, we may want to construct

The Astrology of Local Space

secondary charts for the various localities where the individual has lived or travelled. These charts are equivalent to ones cast for this locality at the time of birth, as if one were born there. This involves a transformation of the radix positions as well as the more familiar shift around the angles of these positions.

Planet on an Angle

Aside from the initial direction from the radix of the locality shift, there are other factors to note. Thru a shift in locality, a planet (or even a city) may be brought onto (or away from) the horizon or an angle. I have found that a planet achieves high focus when on

The Astrology of Local Space

the horizon, in terms of its activity within the individual. In other words, we can adjust and tune our radix -- and ourselves -- thru locality shifts, much like we might tune a musical instrument. This amounts to an adjustment in space rather than over time.

Another objective that might be accomplished by a locality shift is to bring a yet farther away city to high focus -- say to an angle or in aspect to a planet, allowing a second locality shift to be made in its direction. This alters or modifies the psychic interaction of person and place by altering the direction of approach to it. The effect achieved would be quite other than that invoked by approaching it direct. Some of the magical quality of this LS dimension can be seen in the checkerboard-like world concept that emerges, where individuals not only move in relation to a planetary energy they require, but are ever adjusting and jockeying into position to achieve the most resonant move.

The Astrology of Local Space

A Progression in Space

Apart from the focus achieved thru the angles and planets, we may compare aspects and whole-chart patterns with the radix local space chart, considering changes in orientation, and so forth. Another point of interest which has proven very useful in my work is examining the aspects that the planetary positions in the local space locality shift make to the radix local space chart, in particular by bringing one planet to a conjunction with another.

As Charles A. Jayne has pointed out to me, this amounts to a progression of the chart thru space rather than time (a very elegant concept) for those of

The Astrology of Local Space

us, perhaps, who find it hard to wait! I have found that both the conjunction and opposition (the alignments) as formed by this progression in space, are the most significant.

Sun Conjunct Venus

Here I include an example of this "progression in space" to illustrate this beautiful concept. In most methods of progression or direction, a planet such as the Sun, is moved thru time to a conjunction (for example) at another planet's position in the radix. The Sun may be brought to a conjunction with Venus using any of a number of methods to progress or direct a natal chart, and this Venus/Sun conjunction

The Astrology of Local Space

will be precise or exact at some particular moment in time. We may, for instance, look forward to our Venus/Sun conjunction in the 63rd year of life, and so on. Using local space techniques, we may be able to achieve this same Venus/Sun conjunction by means of a locality shift that would bring the Sun to conjunct the local space radix for Venus... in almost no time!

Fine Tuning

Perhaps modern man is developing an intuitive sense for self-adjustment and focus thru locality shifts -- something that ancient man did very little of. It appears that one can enrich and complement various qualities of the radix thru location adjustment --

The Astrology of Local Space

bringing out needed energies at one place and time, moving elsewhere for another life episode at another time. These are some of the fundamental ideas with which I have worked thus far. The obvious value of these charts in the astrologer/client relationship should be clear. I have used these charts with success, and have found that many people are concerned with where they might live in order to bring their self into some resonant and satisfying focus.

The Astrology of Local Space

Article II: Discovering Local Space

There seem to be at least several distinct levels or dimensions to our life and depending upon the clarity of the day, our awareness may be centered in a dimension ranging from the very mundane on up thru an occasional sharing in some sort of more transpersonal or cosmic form of consciousness. It is becoming clear to this astrologer that this multi-dimensionality of our life perhaps may best be represented and examined thru a series of astrological charts, and that an attempt to extract all levels of our life -- the many quite different dimensions

The Astrology of Local Space

– solely from the geocentric ecliptic chart alone is bound to be a frustrating experience. In a word it is: un-necessary.

Ecliptic Coordinate System

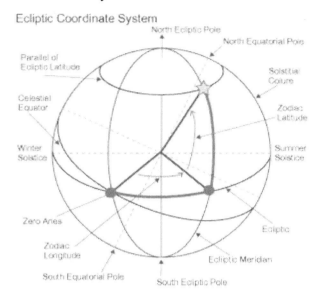

The Zodiac or Ecliptic System

In fact, astrologers make regular use of three very different systems of coordinates (whether they are aware of it or not) each time they erect a natal chart: namely, (1) the zodiac or ecliptic, (2) the equatorial system (right ascension and declination), and (3) the horizon system of coordinates. The actual distinctions between these different systems of coordinates are lost to most of us, and they are kind of jumbled together to form some kind of zodiac pie. It has

The Astrology of Local Space

become my realization that these basic physical planes of reference -- the horizon, equator, ecliptic, and even the galactic and supergalactic planes -- correspond symbolically to the various different dimensions or levels of our consciousness -- as they exist NOW, in their mutual interpenetration.

Furthermore, these levels can be sorted out, and as astrologers we may learn to read these different levels as separate, yet related and whole dimensions of our experience.

Horizon Coordinate System

The Horizon System of Local Space

Let me rephrase all of this. Our Universe, and therefore our Life, can be described or expressed in

The Astrology of Local Space

astrological terms using any one (or all) of several fundamental planes of reference: the Ecliptic, Horizon, Equator, etc. These different planes and their respective coordinate systems are like different languages (or algebras) in that they each can express the same moment in time, the same planets -- in fact, each can express the entire universe, and yet each orders these same objects and data in a different way so as to bring out and raise a particular dimension of reality above the general threshold of our life and into our awareness.

Since our life and consciousness appears to flow thru at least several quite distinct levels, it is my conviction that the most sensible method by which to express or map these different levels is thru these fundamental ordering or reference planes. As astrologers, our almost exclusive concern for the plane of the earth's orbit -- the familiar ecliptic or zodiac -- and the relation of all activity to this plane results for us in a loss of contrast and dimensionality that the use of these alternative coordinate systems might provide.

The Astrology of Local Space

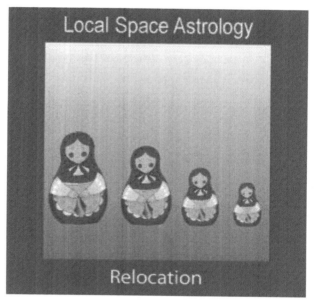

Local Space Astrology

Relocation

As Above, So Below

There are at least two basic factors to consider when examining the various coordinate systems available to us, and they are summed up in the familiar axiom, "As Above, So Below, yet after another manner." The first factor, "As Above, So Below", is an indication that the various coordinate systems may be ordered to form a hierarchy in terms of a progressive "inclusivity", or greater comprehensiveness. In other words, the galactic coordinate system includes the heliocentric within itself, the heliocentric includes the geocentric, the geocentric includes the horizon, and so forth. This represents the "As Above, So Below" portion of the phrase, and this "wheels within wheels within wheels"

The Astrology of Local Space

concept is well understood, and a popular one thru which to express the various dimensions of consciousness. In other words, a large frame of reference or coordinate system somehow involves information of a larger or more meta-physical kind when considered in relation to a more particular or less inclusive system.

"Yet After Another Manner "

The second factor to be illustrated in the phrase, "As Above, So Below, *yet after another manner*" while of equal importance is less well understood. The great reference planes and their respective systems of coordinates are not only inclusive of one another (that

The Astrology of Local Space

is, larger and smaller in relation to each other), but they are also *inclined* at different angles or attitudes to one another. In other words, learning to use and understand the nature of a more inclusive system such as the ecliptic or zodiac system, in relation to the equatorial or "right sphere" system, is not only a matter of ordering the information along a different plane (taking a larger view or picture), but also involves a fundamental change in attitude, or inclination. This shift in attitude, or reorientation of attitude, is an important concept for astrologers to consider and to absorb.

The Astrology of Local Space

Expanded Consciousness

Let me present an analogy which might relate to interpreting these various planes in our everyday life. As a society, we are becoming ever more aware of the cosmic or transpersonal perspective as being associated with the idea of expanded consciousness, with a more whole-view, etc. Yet we have not understood on this same broad social level that such a change in scale or scope may also involve a basic change in attitude: a fundamental change in the approach to life – our inclinations.

The Astrology of Local Space

Change in Attitude or Approach

In other words, growing up is not just a process of taking an ever more inclusive approach, it can also involve a change in attitude or perspective. We can no longer be inclined in directions we once were, and this must amount to a radical change -- that is, change at "root" level -- in our activity! Furthermore, a basic misunderstanding as to what is involved in spiritual growth has resulted from an attempt to view such growth exclusively as some kind of "enlargement." We wistfully look forward to someday growing beyond the particular terms of our everyday existence.

The Astrology of Local Space

This is a result of ignorance of the change in attitude -- the change in point of view, or vantage point -- that accompanies true spiritual development: a change very difficult to imagine or assess for one not aware that such change is a natural and expected part of any deeper initiation.

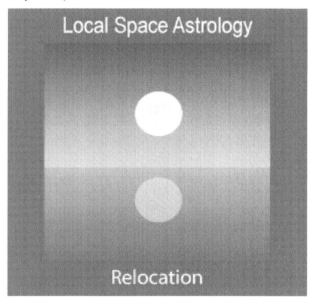

Inclinations and Attitudes

So much for metaphysics. Much of my own research has revolved around these various coordinate systems and the actual dimensions of life they describe. In particular, I have been concerned with the inclinations or attitudes of one system to another. I like to tell myself that the reason for this interest may

The Astrology of Local Space

be due to the fact that I was born with such a "bad" attitude toward some facets of life in this world that vast changes in attitude on my part have been necessary simply for my survival. Let me repeat: these different coordinate systems are great languages or orderings of our total reality and each one raises to our attention its characteristic gestalt or whole dimension of life.

To my knowledge, L. Edward Johndro was the first modern astrologer to make a life-long concern of the articulation of the difference between whole coordinate systems (ecliptic and equator). And in my opinion, a final assessment of Johndro's work may not deal so much in terms of his technical genius alone as with the scope and comprehension of his vision, and in particular, that focus of it relating to the essential differences between events as interpreted on the ecliptic or on the equator. In recent years, this research has been carried on and developed further by Charles Jayne, Theodor Landscheidt, and others.

The Astrology of Local Space

Local Space Astrology

My particular research has centered on the difference and relationship between the geocentric and heliocentric ecliptic systems and, in recent years, on questions of cosmic structure, in particular on an attempt to assess the interpretive meaning of the galactic and supergalactic planes as they stand in relation to one another, and to the zodiac. With these ideas in mind, we are ready to examine a most particular and fascinating system of coordinates: that of the local horizon. There is no intention here to document or "prove" the validity of this system in this very preliminary article. My purpose is to present the impression I have formed regarding the dimension of

The Astrology of Local Space

our life I have found to be mapped in the chart of local space, and to provide those interested with the means to calculate such charts. I would very much appreciate feedback and comments from those of you who investigate this very interesting dimension.

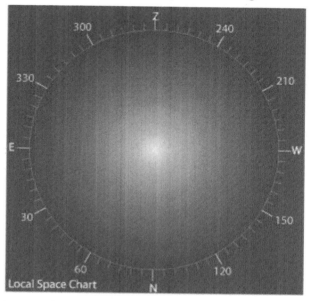

Local Space Chart

Local Space Chart

In simple terms, the local space chart is a map of the 360 degrees of horizon surrounding an event such as birth, much as I might look around us toward the East, West, North, and South. In this horizon coordinate system, the fundamental plane to which all else is referred is the local horizon of the observer, and the position of the various planets as they appear from

The Astrology of Local Space

this location are projected onto the horizon using the familiar astronomical coordinates: azimuth and altitude. Azimuth is the equivalent of zodiac longitude in this system and is measured, for our purposes, from the East direction, thru the North and on around in a counter-clockwise direction -- in the same way that we measure the traditional signs and houses. The Local Space chart wheel is as if one were standing in the northern hemisphere facing South.

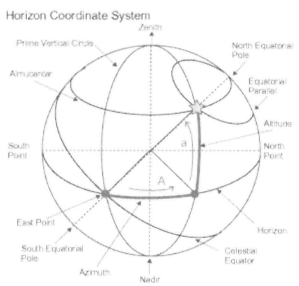

Horizon Coordinate System

The Magic Circle

Altitude, analogous to ecliptic latitude, is measured above and below the horizon to the poles (Zenith and Nadir) from 0 degrees to 90 degrees. It is worth the

The Astrology of Local Space

emphasis of repetition to stress that, from the standpoint of the local space chart, the horizon is the whole azimuthal great circle as it ranges around the wheel of the chart -- not simply the line described by the astrologer's house cusps the First House and the Seventh House, as our astrological habituations tempt us to think. This, then, gives a sort of "flat earth" perspective, as it were, the visible horizon being much like the traditional magical circle. And, as tradition teaches us regarding the nature of the magical circle: the circle is realized to be the equator of a sphere which extends above and below the plane of the local horizon (the apparent or rational horizon cut the infinite sphere in coincident circles).

The Astrology of Local Space

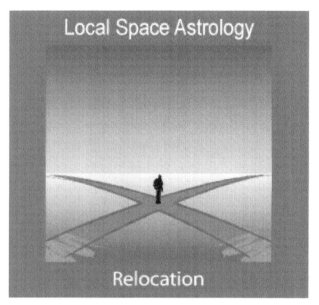

Topocentric View

In this system we have a map in space of an event from a topocentric perspective, from a local center, and thus, an astrology of "local space."

Before I dive into the astrological techniques useful in this new dimension of local space, here is my impression of what Local Space is all about - the general feeling of what portion of life is captured thru this horizon coordinate system.

The Astrology of Local Space

Heaven and Earth as Interchangable

The most remarkable factor, and the key concept you
may need in order to appreciate the particular quality
of the local space chart is to know that every object in
the universe -- whether celestial or mundane -- has an
equal and valid position in this chart. Not only the
planets and stars, but on an equal basis, cities,
countries, and even the local water tower or the
neighbor's house can be represented. All that
concerns us here is the direction of any object in
space -- not their distance. In other words, the
celestial sphere and the mundane or geographic
sphere exist side by side and are interchangeable! A
star is a city is a neighbor. We can walk toward, write

The Astrology of Local Space

letters to, or get up and move into -- for instance -- our 7th house. Even more startling, we can travel toward our natal planets, since they also represent a direction on the globe in the chart of local space.

The Astrology of Local Space

Local Space Techniques

Here then, are some specific approaches I have found to be most useful in examining these charts.

The following remarks represent the most useful technique that has evolved from my research into local space. Space here permits neither a gradual presentation of this information nor the history of, or sequence through which I arrived at these thoughts. Any technique is the very essence of a much larger experience, and every statement here should be investigated and tested out with local space charts in hand.

The Astrology of Local Space

Once you have mastered the mathematics (programs that calculàte local space charts are available from Matrix Software for most popular computer brands) involved in erecting these charts, and have laid them out on 360 degree wheels similar to those pictured herein, a probable series of questions you want to investigate may arise. Let us consider some of them.

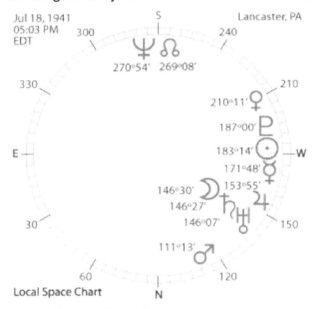

Jul 18, 1941
05:03 PM
EDT

Lancaster, PA

Local Space Chart

Local Space Positions

Compare the planets in the local space chart with your geocentric natal chart. As you will soon note, the individual aspects between two planets can be very different in the two kinds of charts. Also, the larger whole-chart patterns may indicate a different quality,

The Astrology of Local Space

one from the other. A planet may achieve great focus in the local space chart that is not brought out in the Geo chart, and yet you may have intuited and sensed the added importance of this planet or principle in the make-up of the individual involved and yet had no astrological basis for your intuition.

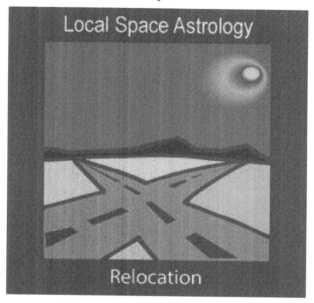

Local Space Astrology

Relocation

Relocation in Local Space

The single most important use of local space in the astrologer/client relationship in my experience has been in locality shifts - relocation. One of the most frequent questions asked this astrologer during a reading is: "Where would be a good place for me to live?" I have made use of the quite valid and useful

The Astrology of Local Space

traditional technique of adjusting the RAMC of the radix to the new locality and coming up with a new Ascendant, set of house cusps, and so forth. The radix positions then are read in terms of these new angles. Local space is by nature suited to express both celestial and geographic positions on one map or chart. Its special nature introduces several concepts not encountered in other techniques.

The Astrology of Local Space

Radix Local Space Charts

Aside from the planetary aspects, there are two primary indicators of strong or high focus in the natal local space chart:

(1) A planet is on or near the horizon (it has low altitude).

(2) A planet is conjunct to one of the four angles or cardinal directions.

It is worth noting which of the planets is closest to the horizon, even if not conjunct. I have used standard orbs for azimuth -- although I haven't arrived at any final rules in this respect. It is also worth noting which

The Astrology of Local Space

planet is most elevated (has the greatest altitude). And the parallels and contraparallels also need investigation.

Cities and Lines

We are now ready to examine a technique that gets to the heart of what these charts are all about. At this point I have in front of me my radix local space chart, with the various planets plotted on it. As I mentioned earlier, we can also plot the positions of cities and places on the earth on this map, so, our next project then will be to translate all of the important cities in our lives into their equivalent positions on our radix map of local space. We should be sure to include not

89

The Astrology of Local Space

only the places we ourselves have lived in or visited, but also the cities that we have always thought that we might like to visit -- that bring a warm feeling to mind, and so forth, not to mention the positions of cities where friends and no-so-friendlies live, where there are business relationships, where packages and letters come from and go to, etc.

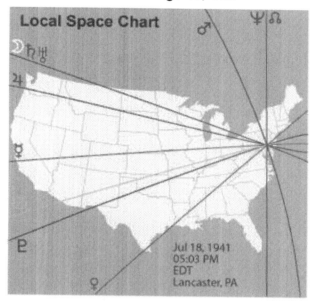

What To Look For

We then examine these various places in terms of their position (or direction) on the local space chart with these thoughts in mind:

Are these cities in aspect, in particular by conjunction or opposition?

The Astrology of Local Space

Are they in alignment with planets in the chart?

In what quadrants and houses do these cities fall?

And are any on the angles?

I have found that individuals tend to move toward cities that are also in the direction of planets that represent the particular kind of energy they may require at that time. An individual, for instance, needing to invoke the key to success often obtained thru Jupiter, may make one or several moves in that direction.

Local Space Astrology

Relocation

The Astrology of Local Space

Mapping the Birth Moment

Although its concept is so simple as to be almost embarrassing, this technique has shown itself to be of great value. In any case, its value seems to be substantial rather than hypothetical. Next to, for example, some of the cumbersome and ultra-traditional place rulerships, proposed national birth-charts, etc. -- many of them seemingly very arbitrary -- the complex and confusing juggling of all these factors seem a rather specious approach to the locality problem, and their results rather tentative.

The local space chart is one of several valuable charts or mappings of the birth moment. As mentioned earlier, it is becoming clear to many astrologers in these times that our life may perhaps best be represented and examined through a series of astrological charts, and that an attempt to extract all levels of our life -- the many quite different dimensions -- from the geocentric ecliptic chart alone is bound to be a frustrating experience. In a word it is: UN-necessary.

The Astrology of Local Space

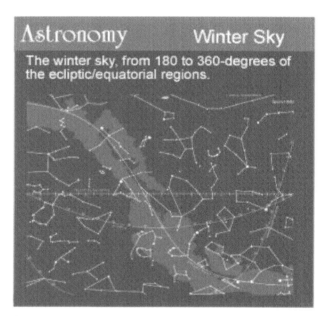

Astronomy — Winter Sky

The winter sky, from 180 to 360-degrees of the ecliptic/equatorial regions.

Out There

I would like to share a few experiences and thoughts with you concerning some of the structure in space beyond the zodiac and how it can be of value in individual development and growth. Let me relate a personal story as to how I first got interested in the deeper regions of space. My own research, as some of you may know, has centered on the difference and relationship between the geocentric and heliocentric ecliptic systems. My interest in the space surrounding our solar system was minimal. I was put off by the billions of stellar objects out there and, on a more basic level, by the ideas of coldness and blackness I had been programmed to associate with outer space.

The Astrology of Local Space

Distant space somehow represented the epitome of other-ness and foreign to me. I was embarrassed, in terms of astrological usage, by all of the books I had read on the fixed stars with the exception of L.E. Johndro's book, "The Stars: How and Where They Influence." How was I to determine the significance of these billions of stars and use them in my practice, when I had enough difficulty, as it was, just using the nine planets and the Sun and Moon?

I Had a Dream

And then the unexpected happened. I had a dream, a very special dream. It was not an ordinary dream, but one of those dreams that are more real than waking

The Astrology of Local Space

consciousness -- that take months to understand and absorb. In my dream the astrologer L.E. Johndro appeared to me and his eyes were filled with light. In fact, there were rays or stalks of light coming out of his eyes. This strange being said but one word, "LOOK!" and with his arm turned and pointed to the Night Sky. I looked. The sky was filled with brilliant points of light. The stars and all of this starry material were clustered together to form the great glowing arch of the Milky Way or galactic plane. It was wondrous beyond description and in that instant my heart went out from me and filled this bright space. Never again have I had the feeling of being here on earth, warm and trembling before the cold and black of space. I became the space and light and reversed my polarity or attitude. I realized that I was a living representative of this mother galaxy. I was the outer spaceman we are all looking for or waiting to find us!

The Astrology of Local Space

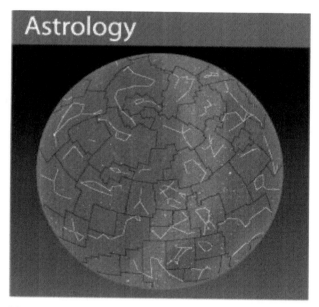

Astrology

Mother Universe

From that night forward I began to venture beyond the zodiac in an inquiry as to the nature and structure of this mother universe. Here, in brief form, is what I found for myself:

We are in fact living nodes or information aggregates. Moreover, the universe is in intimate contact with itself thru us. The many fold nature of the great cosmic events is represented thru our own self and lives. There is not only a correlation between these seeming remote cosmic events and our person, but an identity as well. Information coming from the Galactic Center, carried by electromagnetic and

The Astrology of Local Space

gravitational radiation from every last star and cosmic plane and event, passes thru us at all times. We are, in some way a node or information complex caught in a matrix or web of manifestation.

We Are the Spaceman

The overpowering idea that occurs when we make some acquaintance with the universe and its structure is that there is no difference between out there and in here. We are already out there! Our world and our self and relationships are a perfect reflection of what is and what is happening out there. Not an analogy, but an identity. Black holes, supernovae, quasars, and the like are not only remote cosmic events, but this

97

The Astrology of Local Space

identical story is represented, reflected, lived, and acted out each day in our lives here on Earth.

Information circulates thru the universe and our Identity or sense of our self is this very process of circulation. Identity is not a substance but a relationship, in fact, a circulation and a process of communion or communication. Not only is there a connection between our life and that life of our Galaxy and universe, but: *we* are the connection.

Astronomy — Summer Sky

The summer sky, from zero to 180-degrees of the ecliptic/equatorial regions.

The Symbol is Real

A study of the structure of the universe, at any level, is a study of ourselves, of our life. The guidelines of cosmic structure only help to illustrate the specific

The Astrology of Local Space

structure of our self. In summary, the idea that I am elaborating here is: astrology is not only a symbolic system of psychological discussion. The symbol is also, in fact, real. If we say it is an analogy, then the analogy is complete down to the limits of any specific example we might chose.

We are all time and space travelers. There are no better words that I know of than these of Emerson:

"All inquiry into antiquity is the desire to do away with this wild, savage, and preposterous 'There' or 'Then', and introduce in its place, the 'Here' and the 'Now'. Belzoni (an archeologist) digs and measures in the mummy-pits and pyramids of Thebes until he can see the end of the difference between the monstrous work and himself. When he has satisfied himself, in general and in detail, that it was made by such a person as he, so armed and so motivated, and to ends to which he, himself, should also have worked, the problem is solved, his thought lives along the whole line of temples and sphinxes and catacombs, passes thru them all with satisfaction, and they live again to the mind, or are NOW." -- Essay on History.

The Astrology of Local Space

Discovering Your Self

A process of self-discovery awaits those who would
inquire into the nature and structure of this universe.
We may read and study the history and record of
astrology thru all of the books we have. We may
return again and again to our favorite passages to
make sure of what we have found there. But, sooner
or later, each of us must turn away from the book and
just live. We must ourselves become the book and
only that lives which we have known for ourselves to
have life, which we have lived. There is great value in
a reading of the ancient wisdom and documents.
What the ancients saw or discovered about
themselves, the truth, is still true today. All of the law

The Astrology of Local Space

of the universe still exist to be known today, otherwise how could it be the law? We are always free to leave off at reading about our life and cast off into an inquiry... our inquiry... and to live that life. We can learn to know what we are talking about.

The Astrology of Local Space

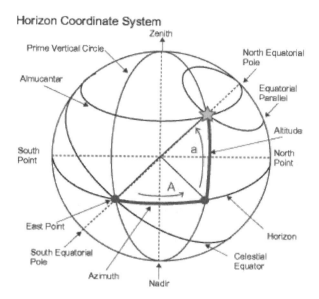

Horizon Coordinate System

Horizon Coordinates

The Horizon System

In the Horizon system a plane through the observing point parallel to the horizon is the plane of reference. The poles are the Zenith (point overhead) and the Nadir (point underfoot). The vertical circle through a celestial object (such as a star) and the zenith is the Object Circle. The coordinates are given (for the object) by Azimuth, which is the horizontal angle (A in the diagram) measured from an arbitrary reference direction -- East in our case -- counterclockwise to the object circle) and the Altitude (a), wich is the elevation

The Astrology of Local Space

angle measured upward from the horizon to the object). The great circle through the north and south points and the zenith is the Meridian, and the great circle through the east and west points and the zenith is the Prime Vertical. Circles of parallel altitude to the horizon that are not great circles are called Almucantars.

Horizon Sphere -- A heavenly sphere based on the plane of the observer's local horizon (90° from both the zenith and the nadir), but taken from the center of the Earth.

Zenith -- The zenith is the point directly overhead any spot on Earth.

Nadir -- The nadir is the point directly beneath (opposite the zenith) any spot on Earth.

Altitude -- The angular distance of any body above or below the plane of the local horizon. Altitude is measured from 0° to 90° from the plane of the horizon to either pole.

Azimuth -- The angle measured around the 360° circumference of the horizon, either east or west (there are different practices). The azimuth of an object as measured from the meridian plane of the observer and a vertical plane through any body.

The Astrology of Local Space

Prime Vertical -- A great circle passing through the zenith (north pole), nadir (south pole), and the east and west points on the horizon.

Altitude Circles -- Parallel circles of altitude, wither north or south of the plane of the horizon.

Almuncantar -- Parallel circles of altitude, wither north or south of the plane of the horizon.

North Point -- A point on the horizon to the north of the observer, where the meridian plane intersects the horizon.

South Point -- A point on the horizon to the south of the observer, where the meridian plane intersects the horizon.

East Point -- A point on the horizon to the east of the observer, where the prime vertical plane intersects the horizon.

West Point -- A point on the horizon to the west of the observer, where the prime vertical plane intersects the horizon.

The Astrology of Local Space

Looking at Local Space Charts

Relocation Example

In the lower right of the above diagram you can see the red dot that marks Lancaster Pennsylvania, my birth place. In this map, Michigan and Pennsylvania are highlighted in yellow. Various cities are labeled.

In addition there is a blue line which marks my natal Jupiter line in Local Space and a red line which marks my Moon-Uranus-Saturn conjunction.

Note that the Blue Jupiter line runs near Ann Arbor, as well as pretty much right through Lansing and

The Astrology of Local Space

Grand Rapids. My first major move after my birth was to Ann Arbor, Michigan, very close to my Jupiter line, about 1.6 degrees.

Jupiter has to do with how we make our way through life's obstacles (Saturn), our particular path or vocation. It was in Ann Arbor that I found my vocations as an astrologer, a musician, and an archivist.

So, you will want to take a look at the Jupiter line in your own natal chart and Local Space map, to see what cities or areas of land it passes through. As for how close or far from the line makes sense, don't always look for or expect to find tight orbs. The real question to ask is which planetary line is the town you are living in nearest to? Of course if it is 90 degrees or more from any line, that won't do. My point here is that Jupiter runs close to Ann Arbor, Michigan, and even closer to Lansing and Grand Rapids.

This suggests that both Lansing and Grand Rapids would also be good for determining my vocation, and there are other factors to consider, like the nature of the town or city itself. Both Ann Arbor and Lansing are major university towns, while Grand Rapids is not. Everything should be factored in, just like it is in day-to-day life.

The Astrology of Local Space

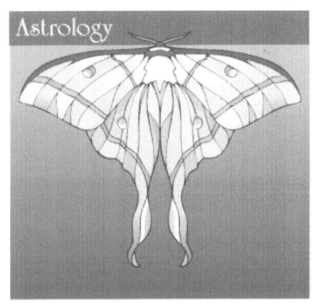

Moon Sign

It was in Ann Arbor, that I really dug into astrology, not to mention entering astrology as a full-time profession. As mentioned earlier, I also found a vocation (for some seven years) as a professional musician, and turned an avocation for interviewing other musicians and artists, which later morphed into an interest (and vocation) in archiving data on music, film, rock posters, and so forth.

As for Lansing and Grand Rapids, Lansing is the home town of my best friend and Grand Rapids is the main town I do most of my larger-item business in, the nearest major city to Big Rapids, where I live.

The Astrology of Local Space

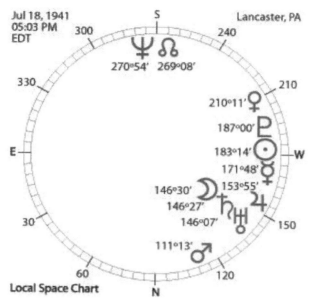

Local Space Chart

Natal Local Space Chart

Now, let's back up a bit and take a careful look at my natal Local Space chart for Lancaster, PA, where I was born. What does it tell me?

A quick look at my natal Local Space chart shows that almost all of the planets (every one except Neptune) are on the Western sides of the chart. If there is some truth to the idea that we tend to move into the direction of our planets, then this brings new meaning to the old phrase "Go west young Man!" I certainly did that.

The Astrology of Local Space

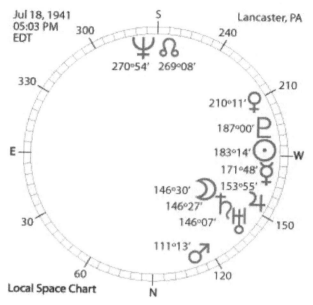

Jul 18, 1941
05:03 PM
EDT
300
S
240
Lancaster, PA

Ψ ☊
270°54' 269°08'

330
210

210°11' ♀

187°00' ♇

E
183°14' ☉
W

171°48' ☿

146°30' ☽ 153°55' ⚷
146°27' ♄
30
146°07' ♅
150

111°13' ♂

60
120

Local Space Chart
N

Southerly Neptune

The most southerly planet is Neptune, but this is also clear from my standard natal chart, where Neptune is on the Midheaven. We can also see that in the Local Space chart, my Sun/Pluto conjunction is tighter, about four degrees in the LS chart, as opposed to 7 degrees in the natal chart.

Perhaps the most interesting fact of the natal LS chart has to do with the triple conjunction of the Moon, Saturn, and Uranus. In my traditional natal chart (geocentric zodiac), the Moon, Saturn, and Uranus are each separate by about three degrees from one another, still quite a tight little stellium conjunction.

The Astrology of Local Space

The Stellium

However in my LS chart, these three bodies (Moon, Saturn, and Uranus) are all conjunct to within less than half a degree, all within about 23 minutes of arc. Now that is a very tight conjunction in anyone's book. What this means is that while in my standard natal astrology chart the Moon, Saturn, and Uranus as seen on the zodiac were spaced apart by some three degrees each.

However, in fact, as seen from my birth place, those three bodies were lined up so that all three were within 23 degrees of azimuth from one another. I other words, had my father walked out and looked at

The Astrology of Local Space

the sky with a telescope, all three of those bodies were one, aligned or conjunct in azimuth (the equivalent of longitude in the Horizon system) exactly. They were lined up in azimuth and stacked one above the other in altitude.

Now this is a significant fact, astrologically speaking, a fact that cannot be seen in the traditional natal chart for my birth. As for how we might interpret it, probably all of us might agree that this close alignment makes this triple conjunction much more important than we might otherwise imagine.

We might also not that Venus and Neptune have the same altitude, and Jupiter is closest to the horizon, a little less than three degrees.

The Astrology of Local Space

	Azimuth	Altitude	
☽	146°30′	-14°26′	**Local Space**
☉	183°14′	+37°35′	**Azimuth & Altitude**
☿	171°48′	+21°37′	Jul 18, 1941
♀	210°11′	+52°57′	05:03 PM
♂	111°13′	-47°45′	EDT
♃	143°55′	-02°46′	Lancaster, PA
♄	146°07′	-10°59′	
♅	146°27′	-07°13′	
♆	270°54′	+52°57′	
♇	187°00′	+46°44′	
☊	269°08′	+52°03′	

Planets at Low Altitude

Planets close to the natal horizon appear to be more important (in greater focus) because of that fact. I always look at the altitudes for the planet to see if any of them are within ten degrees or so of the horizon. If so, then I find them to have increased emphasis in that individual. In particular, the planet closest to the horizon seems important.

In my case, that would be Jupiter, the planet of vocation, literally how we make our way through life. Because it is so close to the horizon, I consider Jupiter to a key factor in my makeup. Also note that both Uranus and Saturn are around ten degrees or

The Astrology of Local Space

less, with Uranus being the next most important, and so forth. So, Jupiter and Uranus are emphasized, pointing to an unusual career. Uranus is considered by some astrologers as the planet of astrology, so we could have that thought as well.

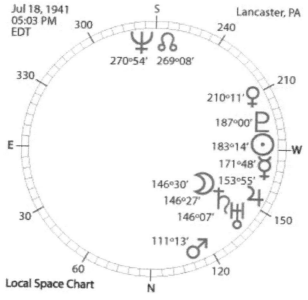

Local Space Chart

Bodies on an Angle

In the LS chart, the four angles are also important, the directions East, South, West, and North. Don't confuse these four directional angles with the more traditional us of the word "angles" to refer to four primary house cusps, First, Fourth, Seventh, and Tenth, although there are obviously related.

The Astrology of Local Space

In my years of work with LS charts, I have found bodies to any one of these four directional points are significant and should be interpreted as such. Looking at my natal LS chart, I have two bodies on angles, Neptune and the Sun. Neptune is the more exact, being conjunct the Zenith direction by less than one degree. And the fact that my Sun is around three degrees from due west is also significant, both by the fact that here we have a body to the angle and also because it is the Sun, which always represents our Self in one way or another. These are both auspicious or significant factors in evaluating this LS chart.

The Astrology of Local Space

Lancaster

Aspect Patterns in the LS Chart

The aspects between bodies in the LS chart have always intrigued me, but never panned out well as for interpretations. In my experience, the aspect patterns in the zodiac in the traditional geocentric natal chart and especially in the heliocentric natal chart are much better indicators than the aspects and their patterns as found in the LS chart. That is just my experience. You may want to explore this yourself.

While simple alignments such as conjunctions and oppositions in the LS chart bring emphasis, I have had less use for the whole-chart aspects and patterns in these horizon charts. This could be due to my own

The Astrology of Local Space

laziness. As an astrologer, I tend to go for the low-hanging fruit with any technique. If I get enough of that to satisfy my curiosity, then I seldom go further. I am not a scholar and seldom do research for its own sake. If I can get a quick picture, that is usually enough for me and looking at the planets to the four angles, alignment by conjunction and oppositions, and altitude (in particular any body close to the horizon) is usually enough for me as regards the LS chart.

However, I do quite a bit with the direction of cities from the natal LS chart and the actual relocation of the LS chart itself.

The Astrology of Local Space

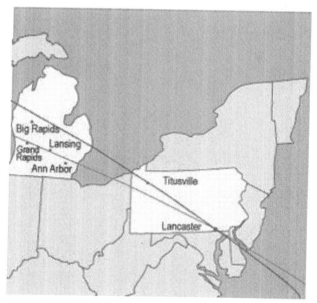

The Direction of Cities

In the beginning, there were no computer programs for LS charts, in fact there were no home computers back then. At that point, although positions in azimuth and altitude had been mentioned in the literature, nothing like a Local Space chart had ever been calculated, much less put forward in an interpretative sense as a legitimate view of a nativity.

In fact, there no calculators with trig functions, at least that I could get my hands on. I had to do my first LS chart using a 4-function calculator and trig tables. I could take me an entire day to do a chart, and each body calculated was cause for some small

117

The Astrology of Local Space

celebration. Gradually I built my own LS chart, planet by planet.

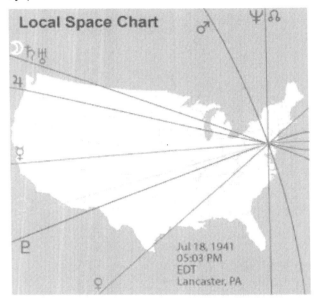

Local Space Chart

Jul 18, 1941
05:03 PM
EDT
Lancaster, PA

Planet Lines are City Lines

Once that was done, I just had to know about the various cities and places I had lived an visited in my life. Where do these places appear in the LS chart? Well, of course I had to figure out how to calculate the direction of cities in Local Space, and then actually do the numbers.

The very first city I calculated the direction for was Ann Arbor, Michigan, which was the main move I had made away from my birth city of Lancaster, Pa. Of course, I was knocked out to find that it was a move

The Astrology of Local Space

directly into my Jupiter, exact to within less than two degrees. In other words, I had moved directly into the primary planet of vocation, literally the guru (Sanskrit word of Jupiter is 'guru') or guide to how we are supposed to get through life. Of course, I wanted to know about some of the other places in my life, so I had to hand-calculate those. The results were equally useful!

My move in 1964 to Berkeley, California to study was a move directly into my Natal Mercury, to within three degrees. Mercury has to do with the mind, with study, and all of that. The other major move I have made in my life is to my present location in Big Rapids, Michigan, which amounts to a move directly into my Moon-Saturn-Uranus conjunction, again a move to within less than 2 degrees of this triple conjunction! More about this later.

The Astrology of Local Space

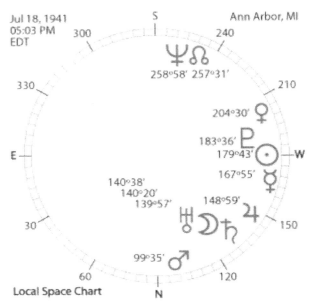

Jul 18, 1941
05:03 PM
EDT

Ann Arbor, MI

Local Space Chart

Relocated Local Space Charts

The next step is to relocate your natal LS chart to the various cities or places you have lived or vacationed in and/or traveled to. This amounts to calculating a LS chart for the same exact date, time, and time zone for when you were born, only using the place coordinates (geographic longitude and latitude) for relocated place. Remember to use the same time and time zone. Everything is the same, except the geographic coordinates. I have an inexpensive program that does all of this for you, if that helps.

Now examine each relocated LS chart using all of the various techniques mentioned earlier. For example,

The Astrology of Local Space

my initial move to Ann Arbor was a move in the direction of Jupiter. In addition, it brings Mercury to one the four angles, the west point. It also positions Uranus to the horizon, by about 1 degree 16' of arc, and Saturn, Moon, and Jupiter are less than ten degrees from the horizon.

Local Space Astrology

Relocation

City Directions from Relocated Charts

One last thing relating to relocated LS charts and that is the direction of cities *from* the relocated chart. In other words, once you have relocated a chart, you may want to know in what direction various cities are from the relocated chart. Compare these city

The Astrology of Local Space

directions to the positions of the new positions of the planets in the relocated charts.

Thus we might relocate along one planet line and then from the relocated chart, relocated again along the relocated planet lines, achieving a move by indirection that might not work out so well as a direct move from the natal LS chart. An example from my own chart.

My initial major move was from my birth place in Lancaster, Pa to Ann Arbor, Michigan, which was along my Jupiter line. It was in Ann Arbor, that I found my vocation. Then I relocated to my current home in Big Rapids, Michigan, which put me on my Moon-Saturn-Uranus line in my natal LS chart. In other words, I found my vocation and then moved to fix that location with Saturn, my Moon-Saturn-Uranus conjunction (less than 30 minutes of arc for all three) is a very powerful part of my natal LS chart.

My move to Big Rapids put Mercury on the West Point, and brought Uranus to 31' minutes of altitude arc from the plane of the horizon, thus positioning Uranus like a laser beam on the horizon. And, although the Moon, Saturn, and Uranus are all less than 10 degrees of altitude, it takes Uranus and selects it out from that tight bunch of three planets. Uranus often represents astrology and also inventive ideas (computers, etc.) of which I have contributed several.

The Astrology of Local Space

Summary of Ideas

In review, let's go over some of the major ways of looking at local space charts.

(1) Bodies on one of the four major angles, East, Zenith, West, and Nadir.

(2) Bodies in alignment by conjunction or opposition.

(3) Bodies within 10 degrees or less of the plane of the horizon.

(4) Direction of cities and places.

(5) Relocated LS Charts, including all of the above points in the relocated charts.

The Astrology of Local Space

(6) Check directions of cities and places in the relocated charts.

(7) Compare positions between natal and relocated LS charts.

The Astrology of Local Space

Relocation Analysis

Now I will go over several relocations using my own chart as an example. Some of you may want to skip over this section, as there is considerable detail. However, for those of you who are trying to understand how to interpreted relocated LS charts, this section should help to spell it out for you.

The Astrology of Local Space

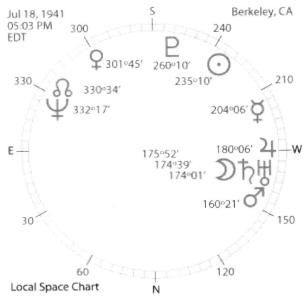

Local Space Chart

Relocation: Berkeley, California

In 1964, I spent a year in Berkeley, studying with a professor there and generally learning more about life. As you can see, the relocated chart for Berkeley does several things. As mentioned earlier, Berkeley is a move directly into my natal LS Mercury. Most important, it puts the planet Jupiter directly on the west angle, exact to within 7 minutes of a degree. This should tell us right off that this place will have a major effect on the life path or vocation, which in fact it did. It opened my eyes not only to astrology, but to all kinds of spiritual inquiry, including the work of Gurdjieff and Ouspensky.

126

The Astrology of Local Space

In addition, I a major spiritual experience of insight, one so strong that it was a transforming event in my spiritual life. Note that Pluto has become in this move the most southerly planet in the chart.

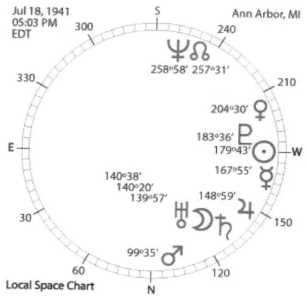

Local Space Chart

Relocation: Ann Arbor, Michigan

We have kind of gone over this, but let's review. Ann Arbor is a move directly into my natal Jupiter, and the move brings the planet Mercury to within three degrees of a major chart angle, the West Point. It keeps Neptune as the most southerly planet. In addition, it places the planet Uranus on the plane of the horizon, with an altitude of 1 degree 16' of arc. It

The Astrology of Local Space

also places Saturn, the Moon, and Jupiter to within less than 10 degrees of altitude on the horizon.

Ann Arbor was where I found several vocations, and where I read just about every major piece of literature in existence, thus the Jupiter and Mercury emphasis. I also became a musician and performed for some seven years, perhaps indicated by the Southerthly Neptune.

The Astrology of Local Space

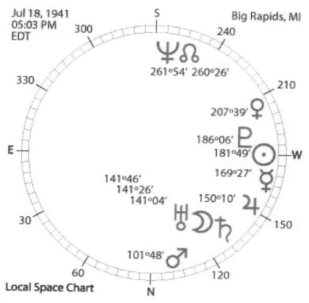

Jul 18, 1941
05:03 PM
EDT

S

Big Rapids, MI

Local Space Chart

Relocation: Big Rapids

As mentioned, this move is onto the line of the Moon-Saturn-Uranus conjunction, perhaps the strongest single factor in my LS charts, since all three bodies are conjunct to within less than 30 minutes of arc. This relocation brings Mercury to about 30 minutes of arc from the west Point chart angle. Another very auspicious effect is that the planet Uranus is brought to within 31 minutes of arc of the horizon, thus singling it out from the Moon and Saturn in that 3-way conjunction. Thus Mercury and Uranus are highlighted, and the entire move invokes that very tight triple conjunction of the Moon, Saturn, and Uranus.

The Astrology of Local Space

Local Space Relocation Astrology

The Astrology of Local Space presents a fascinating method of learning about oneself that involves creating a map of the space immediately surrounding your birthplace. It is very simple. If your mother were to walk outside your home at the moment of your birth, holding you in her arms, and look around, the Sun, Moon and planets would each be in a particular direction from where she stood, whether you could see them at that moment or not.

For example, she could perhaps point toward the direction of the Sun or the Moon in the sky. If we draw a line across the Earth from where she stood in the

The Astrology of Local Space

direction of the Sun, it would pass through any number of cities. Those cities and places mark a path across the earth toward the Sun. You would be examining the space surrounding your locale. This is why I term this technique Local Space Astrology.

Astrology

Formulated in the Early 1970s

The techniques presented in Local Space were developed by me in the early 1970s, before home computers made the scene. At that point, all the calculations had to be done with pencil, paper and log tables. Later I would do them on programmable calculators. This was before the advent of the home computer.

The Astrology of Local Space

What a difference a computer program makes to researchers into local space and its related techniques! The following section is designed to introduce the wide variety of techniques available in Local Space and to sketch out several possible scenarios for personal exploration and research.

Earth Meets Heaven

Astrology is, above all, a way to get to know yourself and your particular orientation to the Earth and the heavens. Here, we will be working with two different sets of maps: geographic maps of the Earth and celestial sky maps. While these maps are very different, they are but different perspectives for

The Astrology of Local Space

graphing the same information. The birth year, date, time and place remain the same. In other words, nothing changes but the coordinate dimension (our perspective and attitude) -- the way we look at this particular piece of time and space.

Celestial = Geographic

When we are working with the geographic maps, we overlay the celestial bodies and the sky map to determine where the planets, stars and other deep-space structure were in relation to places (cities, towns, etc.) on the Earth. We want to find out our particular orientation (attitude) to the cosmos for any given time and place. For example, we know that at

The Astrology of Local Space

any given instant of time, the planet Mars is directly overhead a particular place on the Earth. Local Space allows us to locate just where on Earth that point is.

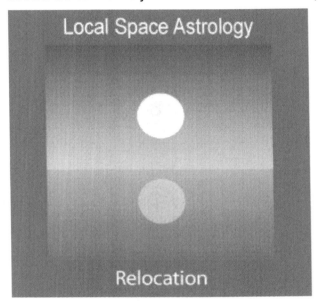

Earth Mirrors Heaven

Local Space techniques bring the heavens down to earth. Planets and stars are no longer somewhere "out there," far off and unconnected objects.

In fact, we exist in a vast web or matrix of connectivity. The planet Earth is set, as a jewel is set, in time and space. As astrologers, we know that all of the various planetary motions are inter-related and synchronized, like some vast cosmic clock. More important, as the Earth turns, it orients or points (from

The Astrology of Local Space

any particular location) first toward one part of the
heavens and then another. At any given time each of
the planets are in a particular direction in space from
where we now stand.

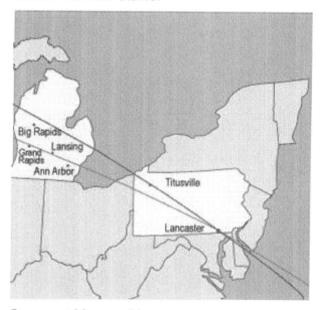

Go west Young Man

Thus the planet Jupiter may be to the west at birth.
Not only is it to the west, but a straight line drawn
from where we stand toward the direction of Jupiter
passes thru a particular series of towns and cities.
These cites are all due west of us. In fact, if we
extend that line, it becomes a great circle stretching
around the celestial sphere. Starting from where we
are, our Jupiter line stretches out toward a particular

The Astrology of Local Space

planet and ends up describing a great circle in the heavens (and on the Earth), returning at last to a point just behind us -- a full 360 degrees. And this entire great circle and the straight line that it describes marks our particular orientation to that great planet Jupiter.

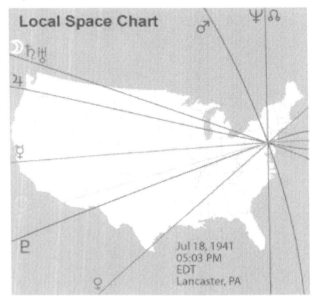

Local Space Chart

Jul 18, 1941
05:03 PM
EDT
Lancaster, PA

360-Degrees

How significant and useful that relation happens to be is up to each of us to determine. I am certain that many people will have no awareness of any connection. Others, like myself, will explore that Jupiter line and learn a lot about ourselves and about our relation to that planet. Jupiter, as astrologers

The Astrology of Local Space

know, is connected to vocational matters, how me make a living, or simply put: the way we go (our path) thru the obstacles of life.

For example, years ago I left my home and moved along my Jupiter line, and took up residence in a town in that direction. It was in that town that I discovered my particular vocation (astrology) and I did not leave that town until that vocation was well set in my consciousness. In other words, I found success in life along my Jupiter line. Later, I moved elsewhere (along other lines) to strengthen and deepen that vocation in other ways.

The Astrology of Local Space

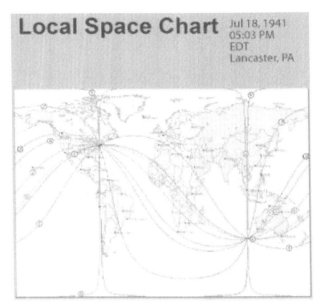

Local Space Chart Jul 18, 1941
05:03 PM
EDT
Lancaster, PA

World Local Space Map

Today, Local Space maps are a built-in part of many astrological programs. Matrix Software, for one, provides these. Others do too.

You will want to enter your complete birth information and check out the local space planet lines (great circles) plotted on a map of the world. This will give you an idea as to what countries and areas of the world (directions) at your birth were oriented toward the various planets. And, since the world is a large place, you will want to zero in on the state or (country) where you were born for a close-up view of all this.

The Astrology of Local Space

State and Local Maps

Make smaller maps for the U.S. and for the state you were born in.

Take your time. Study your particular maps in the light of what cities you have been (or not been) to. And travel is not the only indicator. Where do your friends and not-so-friends live? Where are your business partners? Where have you always dreamed of going? What places do you instinctively not like.

Examine every relation and form of communication you have as regards its direction in relation to your birth map. What does each suggest or tell you? Don't forget to examine planets that are close to the horizon

The Astrology of Local Space

in altitude or near the East, North, West, South compass points.

Horizon Coordinate System

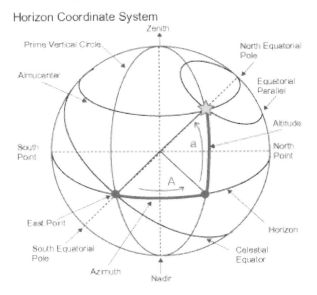

Ways to See Altitude

(1) Out a world or USA map from a program that can produce local space and see how close the planets come to the horizon.

 (2) Another, and perhaps better way to examine altitude is to view a list of LS planets sorted by altitude, with the ones with the least or lowest altitude at the top. Examine the altitude column and see if any planets are less than ten degrees in altitude.

The Astrology of Local Space

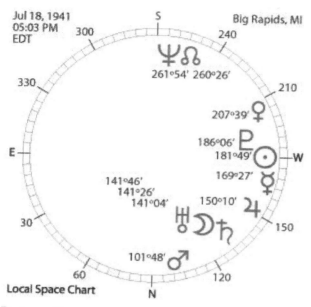

Local Space Chart

Relocation

Next, you will want to relocate yourself to the various other places you have visited and/or wish to go. Again, don't forget to examine the altitude and compass points for planet action. Compare the change in planet strength (Local Space Analysis) from place to place with your particular experience of those places. It will be helpful to look at the local Space chart wheels as well as the maps, since often the altitudes are listed for easy reference.

The Astrology of Local Space

City Directions

And don't forget that one (if not the) most important indication of planet strength is when the city is near the direction of that planet's line on the map. If a planet line runs near a city in question, that a very powerful indicator. What you are exploring is your unique perspective and orientation to the Earth and the heavens -- your particular attitude.

The Prime Vertical

Don't forget to explore the prime vertical coordinate dimension as well. Perhaps, it can wait until you get used to the standard azimuth maps and wheels. Still, keep this dimension in mind. It is every bit as

The Astrology of Local Space

important as the azimuth local space maps. In fact, the prime vertical is the natural complement to the azimuth projection. They are like the cross-hairs on a gun sight. You need both of them to get a fix on your target which is yourself.

Where the azimuth local space chart has to do with action and outreach on our part, the prime vertical dimension has to do with reaction, the response of the world to us. In a word, the prime vertical tells us about that which is fated or destined for us, the areas of life that will happen automatically and don't require effort on our part. The prime vertical charts those areas of life where we can't help but be involved. It is our destiny. None can say no to us where the prime vertical (and vertex) are involved. It is fated.

The Astrology of Local Space

Cycles, Circles, Centers, Circulation

A central idea emerging through my recent cosmic or deep-space research is the use and value of the various astrological coordinate systems (Local Space, Geocentric, Heliocentric, Galactic, etc) as actually best representing the different levels of our life experience. We have been using some of these systems for calculating our astrology charts for centuries, but few of us have thought to extract from them their unique perspectives *interpretively*.

The word CENTER can mean both the same and yet different things to individuals. The center about which our own life appears to revolve is sacred to each of us

The Astrology of Local Space

in its ability to reveal or communicate to us the essence or identity of ourselves, who we are. It is our wellspring or source, our identity.

The center for each of us always refers inward toward our essence, and yet the center or lifeline for one individual may be a new car at one point in their life, a new wife or a child at another point, and so on. However, at each point that center is inviolate for each of us, although the outward form of what we take for our "lifeline to the center" may be constantly changing.

The Astrology of Local Space

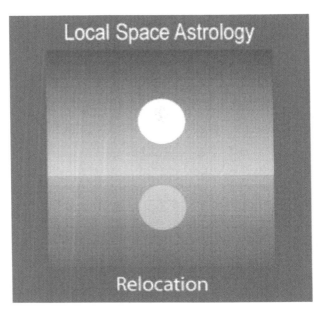

Center as Self

It should come as no surprise to us that the different kinds of "center" may be conveniently expressed in the various coordinate systems of astrology, each of which represents a different perspective on the same given moment in time and space. These different perspectives, each with their individual centers and views, are appropriate or useful for different kinds of inquiry into life.

The particular origin or center chosen for each inquiry should most correspond to the center of gravity, the "kind" of question or inquiry or level being considered.

The Astrology of Local Space

For example, astrology as we know it, combines three
different coordinate systems and planes to arrive at
the traditional natal chart that we all use, the Ecliptic
(Zodiac Longitude and Latitude, the Equatorial (Right
Ascension and Declination) and the Horizon (Azimuth
and Altitude).

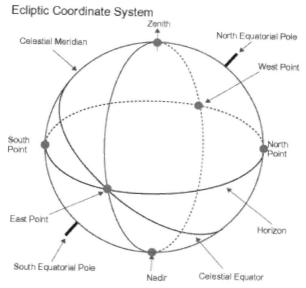

Ecliptic Coordinate System

The Ecliptic or Zodiac System

Although these three (and other) coordinate systems
interpenetrate and are related to one another in
various ways and are used conjointly, they each offer
a very distinct and valuable perspective, when used
alone. Why do we not study these views?

The Astrology of Local Space

Thus for an examination of our personal differences and circumstances, the specific terms of our life (what passes for astrology in most parts of the world), astrologers traditionally use the traditional geocentric astrological chart, with its familiar M.C., Ascendant, houses, etc. In general, Studies of the general terms of mankind (mundane astrology) involve consideration from the center of the earth where we live and work: Geocentric Astrology.

Earth/Sun ⊕ ☉ You / Future

You, the future, what you will become, all the changes you have not yet taken, authority, elders, mentors, men.

Heliocentric or Sun-Centered System

For a study of the motion and relation of the self within the solar system considered as a functioning whole, the Heliocentric Ecliptic System with the origin

The Astrology of Local Space

at the Sun center would be appropriate. In this helio coordinate system, we can examine the archetypes of life and consciousness, and in general questions traditionally referred to religion, perhaps more recently also considered by some as psychological.

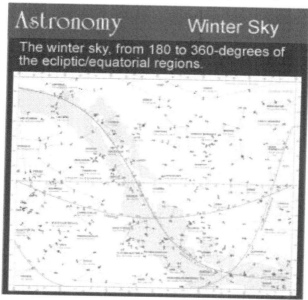

Astronomy — **Winter Sky**

The winter sky, from 180 to 360-degrees of the ecliptic/equatorial regions.

Galactic and Supergalactic Systems

In like manner, Galactocentric and super Galactocentric coordinates are appropriate for dynamical studies of the larger or more cosmic structure of our reality, in particular the direction (or anti-direction) of their centers. For each of us, there may be moments and even days when our awareness is truly of or in synch with cosmic dimensions. After all, it is there. It just may be too obvious or general for us to pick up on. Vast centers are ubiquitous.

Perhaps we could agree that there are different levels of truth or reality. What is essential as a kernel of truth to one may appear to another as one example among many of a larger ordering or structure. When we each refer to our center, the center around which we revolve, we share in the common idea of centers and yet different ones among us revolve around or consider what is central or essential differently. All reference to different centers simply points out the lack of "Identity," and that these seemingly different levels or centers (in fact) form a continuum -- a continuing experience or identification. All centers are linked or shared, somehow.

The Astrology of Local Space

Astronomy   Summer Sky

The summer sky, from 0 to 180-degrees of the ecliptic/equatorial regions.

Large Cosmic Systems

In other words: all of these larger systems such as the Solar System, Galaxy, and so forth include us (here on Earth) within their reaches like a mother holds a child within her womb. We are the children and particular representatives of Earth, and the solar system, but also of the Galaxy and beyond. Their nature, identity, and self (Earth, Sun, Galaxy, Supergalaxy, etc.) is Identical with our own. In fact, we have come up through this "outer space" *through all the time there is* to BE HERE NOW our self.

Our day-to-day consciousness continually circulates from more particular awareness to more "cosmic" awareness and back again. The exercise of various coordinate systems, like exercising our muscles, can serve to remind us that *all* reference to centers (all referral in fact) indicates an attempt to achieve circulation (circle or cycle) or identity, and to "RE"-MEMBER or remind ourselves of who we already are and have always been.

Identification IS Circulation

In other words: all discovery is Self discovery and *identification is circulation*! Cosmic events and cosmic structure are a very consistent and most stable reference frame through which to come to know ourselves. If, in the flux of life, as astrologers,

The Astrology of Local Space

we are looking for a convenient map of our inner and outer experience, we already have it in the various coordinate systems we have always had at hand.

The use of these inclusive (nested) meta-coordinate systems is not the symbolic process some suggest, but here the symbol in fact is real. We are not working with analogies or, if we are, the analogy is complete down to the specific example through which we discover the virtual process itself -- our Life.

The Ends Already Meet

As my teacher taught me, "God" is no beggar, creating a symbolically true but specifically disappointing creation such that we should have to

The Astrology of Local Space

"touch up" his creation or somehow have to make the ends meet. The ends already meet! It is we who will change first our attitude and then our approach to this creation. And these changes in attitude, this reorientation in our approach to what is unchanging or everlasting in life, represent the specific areas where the exercise and use of various coordinate systems of understanding our life become important to present day astrologers. To discover our own orientation and inclination -- that we are already perfect representatives of all space and all time, acting out in detail through our persons events of a so called "cosmic" nature that occur in space at remote distance and times. Is this not what astrology is about?

The Astrology of Local Space

We Are Out There

That we may each discover that supernovae and black holes are not simply some ever-distant cataclysmic events, but are (rather) part of our own everyday experience acted out in fact by persons within the galaxy of our own experience, and that the goal of our study and our inquiry into astrology is to re-present and reveal the nature of ourselves and our intimate circulation and connection and identity in the Heart of the Sun, Heart of the Galaxy, Heart of the Supergalaxy. In a word, and here is the point: the fact that all *identification is simple circulation (a* continuing or circle), and all Inquiry, questioning and search can but end in the discovery of our Self

The Astrology of Local Space

whether "writ small" in the corners of our personal struggle or "writ large" across the very heavens. Again: all self discovery, all Identification is re-discovery and simple: CIRCULATION.

Local Attraction

As we look into the Sun during the course of a year and describe the qualities of those who are born in the various signs, we succeed in defining NOT the position of the Sun, but that of the Earth in relation to the Sun. We all know this.

This illustrates an important axiom: All inquiry into greater centers does not reveal the nature of that center (in itself), but rather reveals our relationship to

The Astrology of Local Space

that center, reveals something about ourselves. In
other words:

Local Space Astrology

Relocation

Centers Serve to Mirror or Rreflect.

Their function is to reveal to us not their intrinsic
nature, but our own. Revelation is (and has always
been) the sign of communication with *greater* centers
or planes. Revelation, not of some far off distant
entity or "God," but always of ourselves and the "God"
in us. We discover the God in ourselves.

In a discussion as to the qualities of the centers of the
Galaxy and Super Galaxy, we can understand that
inquiry into the direction of the Galaxy will serve to
reveal the nature of our own Sun, while inquiry into

157

The Astrology of Local Space

the Super Galaxy will serve to reveal the nature of our Galaxy. The idea presented here is that it is the *nature* of higher centers to reflect and respond to more particular or local centers. Higher centers reflect or show us, ourselves.

Gravity is a Local Pheonomenon

At this point another very significant Axiom emerges. The experience of physical attraction (traction = to draw across or towards) or gravity is primarily a *local* phenomenon. For instance: we directly respond to the attraction we call "gravity," that of the center of the earth. Our Earth responds (by gravity) to the center of the Sun, the Sun to the Galaxy, and so forth. Yet as

The Astrology of Local Space

individuals we are not aware of the pull of the Sun on the entire Earth, much less of the galaxy on the earth, or again: attraction or gravity is always a sign of a *local phenomenon*. This is an important point. Let me explain.

Enlightenment

This perhaps will make more sense in our practical affairs if we put it this way: A sign of our communication with higher or "vaster" centers ("God" or "Total Awareness") is not a physical gravity (graveness) or attraction, but always an *enlightenment*, a releasing and accepting of the nature of the particular terms (terminals) of our

The Astrology of Local Space

existence. Knowledge of so-called inner planes exhibits itself to us through a process of reflection or mirroring of our self rather than through the presentation to us of something new or somehow "other."

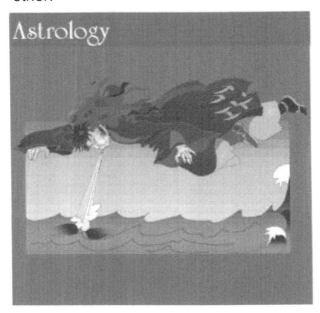

Personal Power

Let me put it crudely, as we might encounter this principle on a day-to-day basis. When I was growing up I was seemingly attracted and drawn into the sphere of all kinds of local power merchants, would-be "gurus" who ruled by their personal power and attractiveness. I, who knew nothing then, lived in terror of these powerful merchants of fear, and

The Astrology of Local Space

struggled to keep from being drawn into an orbit around them. I was foolish enough to think this was what teachers were supposed to look and act like.

Later, when I met my first real teacher, all of this changed, and I could see all of these phonies were no different that I was, struggling to define and assert themselves. What my teacher showed me was not a powerful center around which I was to orbit, but, instead, a kindness and interest in me that I had never before experienced. In fact, my teacher knew how to appreciate and care for me more than I know how to care for myself. In his long-gone reflection I saw myself, and learned something about who I was, not how powerful he was. He had the power to reflect me to myself.

The Astrology of Local Space

Astrology

Higher Centers Embrace Us

From that day forward, I never was fooled by the would-be guru, with their fierce looks and demands. I knew that any real teacher would reflect me and help me to better know myself.

This is what I am trying to say here, when I say that higher centers mirror or reveal to us, reflect our own self, and do not themselves exhibit a greater intrinsic attractiveness or gravity than we (ourselves) already have. In other words, inquiry into centers reveals to us our own essential sense of attractiveness or gravity, not of some "other."

The Astrology of Local Space

In fact, it is the nature of centers, higher centers, to be "non"-material or non-physical, <u>by definition</u>. Our inquiry into this realm of centers is limited only by our fear or reluctance to see our self in this mirror, and seeing through the back of the mirror has always been a sign of Initiation. To sum this up:

Greater centers mirror or reflect our own self and nature, revealing to us our essential identity as already a part of a larger whole, and enlightening us of (or from) our "grave-ness" and the burden of an apparent loneliness or imagined separation from that whole.

These centers are our personal welcoming committee, helping us identify ourselves as already belonging to a line or lineage, stretching back as far as life itself.

The Astrology of Local Space

Higher Centers

With this idea in mind, let us resume our investigation as to the nature of the Galactic and Supergalactic Centers. Given the above, we can expect the Galactic Center to exercise considerable greater physical attraction on our Sun (and ourselves) than that of the local Super Galactic Center. In fact, one of the identifying features of the Galactic Center (GALACTIC CENTER) at work as revealed in chart analysis (research by astrologers Charles Harvey, Theodore Landscheidt) is a certain "macho" like quality, a sense of strength and power perhaps typified in the zeal and self-righteousness of certain extreme religious factions. Or more simply: this

164

The Astrology of Local Space

tendency in the qualities of Sagittarius and Capricorn of sternness and physical action or "power." Everything is already conveniently embedded in the meaning of the common zodiac signs.

Another way to put this is to point out the great ability and power of the Galactic Center as represented (when strongly aspected) in the natal chart to move and attract others. We find this feature in the charts of great political and religious leaders who possess the power to move nations to action. The Galactic Center figures in these charts in the traditional astrological ways -- by conjunctions and other aspects to the Galactic Center. We may contrast this "macho-like" quality found in the Galactic Center to the

The Astrology of Local Space

qualities that indicate the presence of Super Galactic Center (SGC) in natal charts. Here we look to the traditional qualities of Virgo and Libra -- that of care, service, reflection, and love.

Planet Chakras   Mercury

Mercury, an internal planet, is the light in our eyes, the mind itself, clarity, discrimination.

Buddha = Awareness

Perhaps the best representative of the Super Galactic nature occurs in the Eastern religion Buddhism, in the idea of compassion and especially in the beloved figure of the Bodhisattva, a being who is literally devoted to the service of all life until ignorance vanishes in every one in complete identification of self as one with "God."

The Astrology of Local Space

The Galactic Center is located around 26 degrees of Sagittarius. The Supergalactic Center is located around 1 degrees of Libra, roughly at right angles to one another.

We do not find the SGC as physically powerful and moving as we do the GC. In the West, the traditional god figures are more fierce and full of the "fire and brimstone" approach than of the endless care and service as typified in some of the Eastern traditions.

In fact, only in these times we are now living are the "servile" qualities associated with Virgo sun sign coming to be appreciated as a power in themselves. In other words, the SGC represents a non-material or essentially a passive power rather than the more active kind of power as seen in the Galactic Center Idea. In the Bible it repeatedly says "This came to pass... that came to pass." The passive genius, not active in the "doing of things" but rather active in the "undoing of things," that is: helping things to pass from this world. This SGC is a non-material or spiritual task and genius equally to be valued along with the more active One-who-does-things or brings-things-to-be in this world (G.C.). We can see these two archetypes at work in the world, and they may be conveniently studied in their local representatives: the Galactic and Super Galactic centers and planes.

The Astrology of Local Space

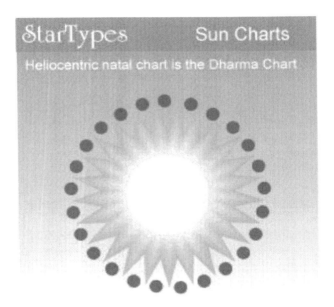

StarTypes   Sun Charts

Heliocentric natal chart is the Dharma Chart

So Inclined

"As Above ,So Below, but After Another Manner," familiar as an occult maxim, might be the perfect description of what is involved in understanding the various astrological coordinate systems and their transformations. It is easy to communicate the concept of "wheels within wheels" (larger systems containing within them nested smaller systems), and this has resulted in the popular idea of the chakras or planes (planets) of our experience and Self as an ascending hierarchy of levels, each inclusive of the preceding level.

The Astrology of Local Space

A Matter

Astrology

Yesterday   Today   Tomorrow

A Matter of Inclination

What is not generally appreciated, but which becomes increasingly clear when we examine the actual structure of the various cosmic systems is not only the idea of larger systems embracing the small systems within them (levels), but the fact that each larger system is also differently *inclined* to the preceding one. It should be understood that aside from the often tedious mathematics involved in coordinate transformations, there is an accompanying philosophical or psychological adjustment to be made,

The Astrology of Local Space

a shift in viewpoint, a change in the approach or attitude to the subject.

So, there is not only an "expansion" in perspective when we move to a larger coordinate system, but there is also a reordering of our sense of direction. This is what makes it so difficult for an individual to see beyond his or her present dimension and get a feel for what is perhaps their inevitable future. There exist what are termed "event horizons," beyond which we cannot understand how life can go on.

Rites of Passage

An example of some event horizons: puberty, marriage, child birth, and death, to name a few of the

The Astrology of Local Space

classics. We cannot see beyond our present sphere into what our future might be like in these other dimensions because we cannot help but conceive of these events in terms of our present line (linear) of thought. To pass through these event horizons involves total change, not just an extension or expansion. We do not watch our own change, for we are what "Is" in fact in transition or change. *We* are changing. As I used to put it to myself: I was wondering what I was going through, until I realized I was going through.

The Astrology of Local Space

Planet Chakras   Saturn

The Saturn experience can be a hard one, something to get through. Confined

Event Horizons

The idea presented here should be obvious: the crossing of an event horizon involves simple reorientation on our part, call it a change of approach or attitude. The new dimension or sphere we enter turns out, after our adjustment or change, to reveal our previous or past life in new light. We see our old behavior and opinions differently in our new approach to life. It may be very difficult, as we all know, to communicate this difference to one who has not yet had that experience. What has changed perhaps most is our INCLINATION. We do not want the same things we did want, or we now want them in a different manner. We are no longer inclined such that

The Astrology of Local Space

we feel the way we used to. Our life now revolves around a different center than before -- a wife or child, for instance.

We not only revolve around a different center or point to a different star, but that amounts to a change in inclination and direction. That change in inclination is what is hard to convey to someone looking to have that experience. We call all grasp the idea that a "greater' experience will embrace our previous experience like a set of Russian nesting dolls. We all get that.

The Astrology of Local Space

Centers and Orientation

What has not been properly presented is that along with the expanded experience and the embracing of what went before is a shift in inclination, a new perspective. If we are studying with an enlightened teacher (from our perspective), we tend to imagine an expanded consciousness, but always in relation to our current center. We don't know, spiritually or psychotically speaking, where a deeper or "greater" center is located, and this by definition. If we did, we would already be oriented.

What the teacher does is very clear in Asian religions, where the teacher gives what are (interestingly

The Astrology of Local Space

enough) called the "pointing out" instructions, after which the student, with some practice in day-to-day life experience, manages to get the "point," and, through an often slow and painful time, manages to reorient themselves to point to the new center. To "get the point" here means to get reoriented.

Everything shifts, and the previous center is no longer considered "central," and either dissolves or looses interest or magnetism for the student. This is the idea of centers we are presenting here, only through the wonderful precision of these natural astrological coordinate systems.

The Astrology of Local Space

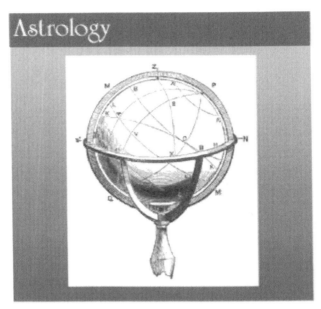

Astrological Coordinate Systems

In fact, many of these principles are graphically revealed through the study and exercise of the various astrological coordinate systems. For instance: what appears in one system as isolated and singular entities that are apparently unconnected, when viewed in the perspective of another system define the basic shape of the system itself. How often in our lives does some singularity appear as if an other and foreign entity, but later, when we have experienced several of this type as representatives of a kind at first unfamiliar, this same event becomes recognizable to us and loses its threatening quality. It happens all the time to each of us.

The Astrology of Local Space

I cannot recommend strongly enough the exercise of these various ways or systems for understanding our universe to astrologers practicing today. Let us examine briefly some of these larger systems and their systems and their Centers. For those of you interested in a more thorough description and catalog of of the various members of these systems see my book: "Astrophysical Directions" (1976).

Cosmic Systems and Centers

1. SOLAR SYSTEM   Center: Sun

2. LOCAL SYSTEM   (Gould's Belt) This is a group of some 10 to the 8th stars of which the Sun is a member. The Local System, originally thought to be a minute galaxy embedded with the Milky Way, is considered to be an ellipsoid of 700x200 parsecs with the long axis parallel to the New Galactic Longitudes 160-deg/340-deg and located in Orion-Cygnus spiral arm. The centroid of the Local System is in Virgo at about 15deg25' with nodes to the Ecliptic at 10deg22' of Sagittarius (North node) and Gemini. The system is inclined to the ecliptic by about 66 degrees. Note – positions are of the Epoch 1950.0.

3. LOCAL GALAXY...The Milky Way. Estimated to contain 10 to the 11th stars, The Galaxy is a disc-like structure with a diameter of some 30,000 parsecs, a central ellipsoidal nucleus of about 4000 parsecs, and an average disc thickness of several hundred parsecs. The nodes and center (about 26-degree of Sagittarius) in relation to the ecliptic are given

The Astrology of Local Space

elsewhere. The Sun is located some 10,000 from the Galactic Center.

4 LOCAL GROUP OF GALAXIES The local group includes about a score of member galaxies...the largest of which is the Andromeda Galaxy (M 31), our galaxy, and M-31 revolve around a common center of mass roughly in the direction of 27-degress in the Sign Aries.

5 LOCAL SUPERGALAXY . Our Galaxy is part of a vast flattened super system of galaxies some 40 megaparsecs in diameter, with the center (at 1 degrees of Libra) in the great Virgo Cluster some 12-16 megaparsecs from our Sun.

The Astrology of Local Space

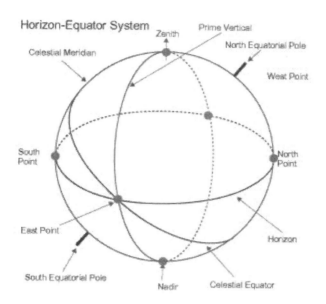

Horizon-Equator System

The following labels appear in the diagram: Zenith, Prime Vertical, Celestial Meridian, North Equatorial Pole, West Point, South Point, North Point, East Point, Horizon, South Equatorial Pole, Nadir, Celestial Equator

The Horizon System

We will return to some additional ideas as to the relationship between the equator and the ecliptic after we introduce the third major astrological system of coordinates, that of the Horizon.

The Horizon system of coordinates represents the third and last of the spherical systems used in constructing a natal chart. In this system, the reference plane is one through the birthplace or observing point that is parallel to the horizon. The poles of this system are the Zenith (point overhead) and Nadir (point underfoot). The latitude-type coordinate in this system is called Altitude and is

The Astrology of Local Space

measured from 0° to 90° from the plane of the horizon to either pole. The longitude coordinate is called Azimuth and is measured from 0° to 360° along the horizon (for astrological use in this book), starting from the East point and moving in a counterclockwise direction through the North point and on around, in the same way that we are used to measuring houses or signs.

The Horizon System is built around the specific place on earth of the event and all other objects, such as planets, stars, cities, etc. are then expressed in terms of how they were oriented or appear from this perspective. The horizon system is most like the standard road map in that it has a North-South-East-West orientation. The North-South axis is identical to the Celestial Meridian running from the north celestial (or geographic) pole through the observer to the south pole. The East-West circle is called the Primer Vertical and runs due East or West from the observer. It does not follow the East-West geographic parallels of latitude. The horizon system can be anyplace on earth you are.

The Astrology of Local Space

The North Star

The Pole Star (North Star)

The earth is endlessly revolving, exposing us, wherever we are, to the entire circle of the heavens. At night, we can see the stars, planets, and constellations, change every few hours or so. But there are two places in the heavens that do not change, and that is the part of the heavens directly above (and below) the north and south geographic poles, respectively. Everything revolves around those two points.

In the Northern Hemisphere, there happens to be a star right above the North Pole, and this is called (obviously) the Pole Star. It is also called the North

The Astrology of Local Space

Star. This star has been used forever as a guide star for travelers and seamen, because it is the one celestial object in the Northern Hemisphere that is always there. It does not change.

The Astrology of Local Space

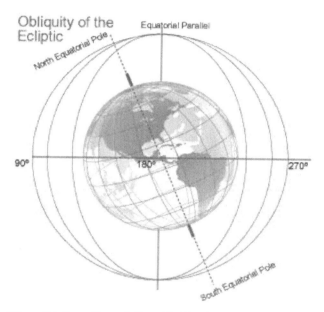

The Obliquity of the Ecliptic

The angle between the ecliptic and equatorial systems, some 23.5 degrees, is called the Obliquity of the Ecliptic, and this angle creates the difference in perspective between the two systems. Let's go over some of the main points of difference between these two systems.

1. The celestial equator and the ecliptic plane intersect to form the two equinoxes and the equinoctial axis.

The Astrology of Local Space

2. The Vernal Equinox or 0° Aries node or point is the ascending node of the ecliptic plane to the equatorial plane.

3. The Autumnal Equinox or 0° Libra point is the descending node of the ecliptic plane to the equatorial plane.

4. These points and these two coordinate systems are FIXED in space.

5. AT ANY MOMENT and AT ANY PLACE in the Earth's orbit, the ZERO° Aries point is ALWAYS in the same direction and at an infinite distance.

6. The measurement of longitude along the ecliptic or the equator is only identical at the four Cardinal points: the two equinoctial and solstitial points.

7. At all other points, there is a difference between a degree of longitude (the same degree) as measured along the ecliptic and the same degree measured on the equator.

8. Each system is simply tilted at an angle to the other.

The Astrology of Local Space

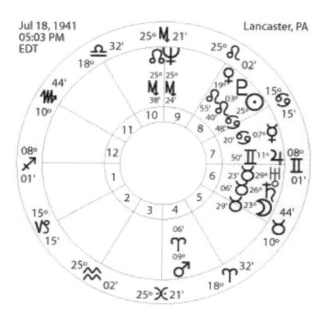

Relocated Angles and Houses

Perhaps the oldest of the three methods involves relocating the natal chart angles and houses, which is as simple as casting a chart for your birth day and time, but for another locality – a different place.

While the angular relationships between the planets (planetary aspects) do not change using this technique, the chart angles (Ascendant, Midheaven, Vertex, etc.) and the house cusps do change. The result is that using this method, you get differing relationships to the angles and particular planets can appear in houses other than in the standard natal chart.

185

The Astrology of Local Space

In other words, you can alter house and angle relationships to the planets, which may enhance and make a particular configuration more prominent or it may de-emphasize a configuration, perhaps putting an inauspicious planet two more to the back burner and away from center stage. Here is a simple example:

Suppose I have Saturn in the 7th House, the house or marriage and public recognition. I may not want Saturn there. By relocating the angles by moving to another town or city, I may be able to push Saturn into the 8th House, where it might be a little more at home, freeing my 7th House up for an easier marriage or what-have-you?

The Astrology of Local Space

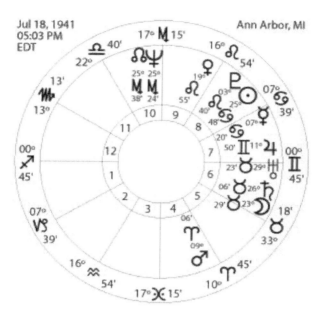

Jul 18, 1941
05:03 PM
EDT

Ann Arbor, MI

Relocation to Ann Arbor, Michigan

The Move to Ann Arbor does a number of things using this technique. Perhaps most important, it brings the planet Uranus directly to the Descendant, the 7th House cusp, thus emphasizing "astrology," computers, and inventions in general. It was here that I became a professional astrology, was the first person to program astrology on a home computer and make those programs available to my fellow astrologers, and also develop a number of innovative techniques, like this one: Local Space.

It brings Mercury to the 8th House cusp, emphasizing esoteric thinking and theory. It also places Venus in

The Astrology of Local Space

the 9th House, rather than the 8th House, making for
an interest in things that last, such as religion, in this
case it was Buddhist mind training that was
undertaken.

The Astrology of Local Space

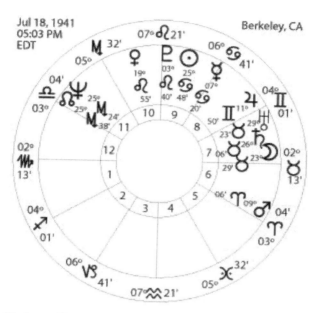

Relocation to Berkeley, CA

My relocation chart for Berkeley, CA gives me a
Scorpio Ascendant, moves mars into the 6th House,
and my stellium of Moon-Saturn-Uranus into the 7th
House. My Jupiter moves into the 8th House, and the
Sun and Mercury move into the 9th. Perhaps most
important, it places Pluto on the Midheaven, and it
was here that I had a number of mind-opening
experiences, most transformative.

The Astrology of Local Space

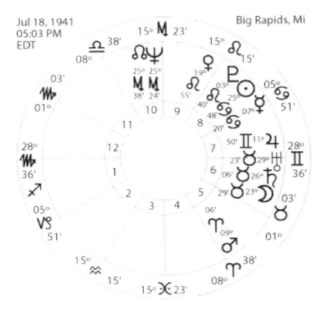

Relocation to Big Rapids, MI

My relocation chart for Big Rapids, MI does several things. It gives me a late Scorpio Ascendant. It puts Mars into the 5th House, a major change, which accents my children and creativity, in general. It places the astrological planet Uranus on the 7th House cusp (Descendant), which also rules computers and innovations. Mercury is moved into the 8th House of the esoteric mind, and Venus is moved into the 9th House of religion, in this case Tibetan Buddhism.

The Astrology of Local Space

The Astrology of Local Space

Astro-Geography

This particular technique, Astro*Geography, was discovered by astrologers Donald Bradley and Gary Duncan, but later popularized under the name "Astro*Carto*Graphy" by astrologer Jim Lewis in the latter part of the 20th Century. It is still very much used today and many astrological programs include it. You can also buy "Astro*Carto*Graphy" maps from various online services.

This is not a book about A*C*G, but since it is one of the three leading methods of astrological relocation, let's go over it briefly to make clear what it is. There are a number of articles and books on Astro*Carto*Graphy available, so look there for further information.

A*C*G using a standard geographic map such as you might find in a road atlas or state map. On this geographic map are draw curved lines that represent where the nine planets, the Sun and Moon are rising at the moment of a birth. In other words, these lines represent all the places in the world where if you were born at this moment, you would have a particular planet rising, that is on the exact cusp of the First House.

A similar line is also calculated for each planet that marks the point the planet where the planet is setting (on the Descendant) or in other words is on the Seventh House cusp. Additionally, lines for the Midheaven (MC) and Imum Coeli (I.C.) are also given.

The Astrology of Local Space

The lines for the MC and IC are always vertical lines running North and South on the map, while the rising and setting lines are always curved lines creating great circles. Thus for the ten most bodies in astrology (nine planets, the Sun and Moon), there would be a total of 40 lines plotted, for each body a rising, setting, and MC and I.C. line.

What Are A*C*G lines?

A*C*G lines (as pointed out above) show all the places in the world you might travel or relocate to, where you would have a First House (or Seventh House) emphasis. In other words, when you are at that location, it is as if you were born there with the particular planet rising (on the cusp of the First House) or setting (cusp of the SeventhHouse), directly above (Midheaven) or directly below (Imum Coeli). Only these four points (for each body) are represented in Astro*Carto*Graphy. The rest of the local horizon is ignored using this method. Here is an example:

The Astrology of Local Space

Planet Uranus in A*C*G

In the above A*C*G map (or a section of it), you can see the Uranus line passing through Michigan. Other rising/setting lines in the U.S. include the Moon, Saturn, and Jupiter. That's it. There are some Midheaven/I.C. lines (the vertical lines) for Venus, Pluto (off the coast), Neptune, and the Lunar North Node, but nothing else. As we will see later on, using Local Space, we can also mark Uranus on the horizon in Michigan, but also what direction (planet line) any city is from the natal/radix chart.

The Astrology of Local Space

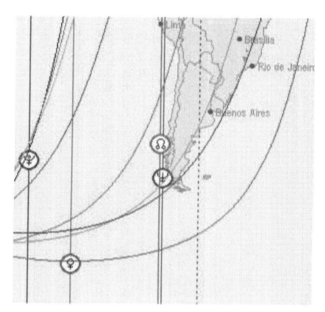

Pros and Cons

On the pro side, A*C*G is very popular and does show where you might achieve angular planetary emphasis – planets rising or setting, at the Midheaven (above) or the I.C. (below).

One of the problems I have with A*C*G is that you may have an important line (let's say the Sun or Venus) that is almost entirely in the middle of the oceans. In the above example, you can see my venus is literally out-to-sea. Not much chance I will ever visit there (except perhaps on a cruise ship), much less relocate there. Is my love life too emotional (water)?

The Astrology of Local Space

The other main problem I have with the A*C*G technique is that it does not tell you in which directions the planets and other bodies are at birth, much less which cities these lines pass through. Luckily the Local Space chart does this, which is what this book is primarily about.

The Astrology of Local Space

Michael Erlewine

Internationally known astrologer and author Noel Tyl (author of 34 books on astrology) has this to say about Michael Erlewine:

"Michael Erlewine is the giant influence whose creativity is forever imprinted on all astrologers' work since the beginning of the Computer era! He is the man who single-handedly applied computer technology to astrological measurement, research, and interpretation, and has been the formative and leading light of astrology's modern growth. Erlewine humanized it all, adding perception and incisive practical analyses to modern, computerized astrology. Now, for a second generation of astrologers and their public, Erlewine's genius continues with StarTypes ... and it's simply amazing!"

The Astrology of Local Space

A Brief Bio of Michael Erlewine

Michael Erlewine has studied and practiced astrology for over 40 years, as an author, teacher, lecturer, personal consultant, programmer, and conference producer.

Erlewine was the first astrologer to program astrology, on microcomputers and make those programs available to his fellow astrologers. This was in 1977. He founded Matrix Astrology in 1978, and his company, along with Microsoft, are the two oldest software companies still on the Internet.

Michael, soon joined by his astrologer-brother Stephen Erlewine, went on to revolutionize astrology by producing, for the new microcomputers, the first written astrological reports, first research system, first high resolution chart wheels, geographic and star maps, and on and on.

Along the way Matrix produced programs that spoke astrology (audio), personal astrological videos, infomercials, and many other pioneering feats.

Michael Erlewine has received major awards from UAC (United Astrological Conferences), AFA (American Federation of Astrologers), and the PIA (Professional Astrologers Incorporated), and scores of on online awards.

Michael and Stephen Erlewine have published a yearly calendar for almost 30 years, since 1969. Michael Erlewine has produced and put on more than

The Astrology of Local Space

36 conferences in the areas of astrology and Buddhism.

Example Astro*Image Card

Aside from his current work as a consultant for NBC's iVillage and Astrology.com, Erlewine has personally designed over 6,000 tarot-like astrology cards, making authentic astrology available to people with little or no experience in the topic. These Astro*Image™ cards are available through a variety of small astrological programs and in eBooks. Some examples can be found at WWW.StarTypes.com, where there is also a link to his astrological software.

The Astrology of Local Space

Michael Erlewine has been doing personal astrology readings for almost forty years and enjoys sharing his knowledge with others. However, his busy schedule makes it difficult to honor all requests. However, feel free to email (Michael@Erlewine.net) him if you wish a personal chart reading. He will let you know if his current schedule will allow him to work with you.

The sections that follow will give you more details about Michael Erlewine and his very active center.

The Heart Center House

In 1972, Michael and Margaret Erlewine established the Heart Center, a center for community studies. Today, the Heart Center continues to be a center for astrological and spiritual work. Over the years,

The Astrology of Local Space

hundreds of invited guests have stayed at the Heart Center, some for just a night, others for many years. Astrologers, authors, musicians, Sanskrit scholars, swamis - you name it, the Heart Center has been a home for a wide group of individuals, all united by their interest in spiritual or cultural ideas.

Heart Center Library

Erlewine also founded and directs The Heart Center Astrological Library, the largest astrological library in the United States, and probably the world, that is open to researchers. Meticulously catalogued, the current library project is the scanning of the Table of Contents for all major books and periodicals on astrology.

The Astrology of Local Space

The library does not have regular hours, so contact ahead of time if you wish to visit. Michael@erlewine.net.

The Astrology of Local Space

The All-Music Guide / All-Movie Guide

Michael Erlewine's devotion to studying and playing the music of Black Americans, in particular blues, led to his traveling to small blues clubs of Chicago and hearing live, blues greats like Little Walter, Magic Sam, Big Walter Horton, and many others. He went on to interview many dozens of performers. Much of this interviewing took place at the Ann Arbor Blues Festivals, in 1969 and 1970, the first electric blues festivals of any size ever held in North America, and than later at the Ann Arbor Blues & Jazz Festivals.

With their extensive knowledge of the blues music, Erlewine and his brother Daniel were asked to play host to the score or so of professional blues musicians and their bands. They were in charge of serving them food and (of course) drink. Michael went

The Astrology of Local Space

on to interview most of the performers in these early festivals, with an audio recorder, and later on with video.

The interviewing led to more study and ultimately resulted in Michael founding and developing AMG, the All-Music Guide, today the largest single database of music reviews and documentation on the planet.

Erlewine started from a one-room office, and the reviewers and music aficionados of the time laughed at his attempt to cover all music. But he persisted, and the all-Music Guide appeared as a Gopher Site, before the World Wide Web even existed-a database of popular music for all music lovers.

Over the years AMG grew, and the All-Movie Guide and All Game Guide were born, and also flourished. Later, Erlewine would create ClassicPosters.com, devoted to the history and documentation of rock n' roll posters, some 35,000 of them.

These guides changed the way music was reviewed and rated. Previous to AMG, review guides like the "Rolling Stones Record Guide" were run by a few sophisticated reviewers, and the emphasis was on the expertise of the reviewer, and their point of view. Erlewine insisted on treating all artists equally, and not comparing artist to artist, what can be important, Michael points out, is to find the best music any artist has produced, not if the artist is better or worse than Jimmie Hendrix or Bob Dylan.

The Astrology of Local Space

Erlewine sold AMG in 1996, at which time he had 150 fulltime employees, and 500 free-lance writers. He had edited and published any number of books and CD-ROMs on music and film. During the time he owned and ran AMG, there were no advertisements on the site and nothing for sale. As Erlewine writes, "All of us deserve to have access to our own popular culture. That is what AMG and ClassicPosters.com are all about." Today, AMG reviews can be found everywhere across the Internet. Erlewine's music collection is housed in an AMG warehouse, numbering almost 500,000 CDs.

Heart Center Meditation Room

Michael Erlewine has been active in Buddhism since the 1950s. Here are his own words:

The Astrology of Local Space

"Back in the late 1950s, and early 1960, Buddhism was one of many ideas we stayed up late, smoked cigarettes, drank lots of coffee, and talked about, along with existentialism, poetry, and the like.

"It was not until I met the Tibetan lama, Chogyam Trungpa Rinpoche, in 1974 that I understood Buddhism as not just Philosophy, but also as path, a way to get through life. Having been raised Catholic, serving as an altar boy, learning church Latin, and all that, I had not been given any kind of a path, other than the path of faith. I hung onto that faith as long as I could, but it told me very little about how to live and work in this world.,

"I had been trying to learn the basics of Tibetan Buddhism before I met Trungpa Rinpoche, but the spark that welded all of that together was missing. Trungpa provided that spark. I got to be his chauffer for a weekend, and to design a poster for his public talk.

"More important: only about an hour after we met, Trungpa took me into a small room for a couple of hours and taught me to meditate. I didn't even understand what I was learning. All that I know was that I was learning about myself.

"After that meeting, I begin to understand a lot more of what I had read, but it was almost ten years later that I met my teacher, Khenpo Karthar, Rinpoche, the abbot of Karma Triyana Dharmachakra Monstery, in

The Astrology of Local Space

the mountains above Woodstock, NY. Meeting
Rinpoche was life-changing.

Heart Center Symbol

"It was not long after that we started the Heart Center
Meditation Center here in Big Rapids, which is still
going today. My wife and I became more and more
involved with the monastery in New York, and we
ended up serving on several boards, and even as
fundraisers for the monastery. We helped to raise the
funds to build a 3-year retreat in upstate New York,
one for men and one for women.

"We also established KTD Dharma Goods, a mail-
order dharma goods business that helped
practitioners find the meditation materials they might
need. We published many sadhanas, the traditional

The Astrology of Local Space

Buddhist practice texts, plus other teachings, in print and on audio tape.

Years have gone by, and I am still working with Khenpo, Rinpoche and the sangha at the Woodstock monastery. Some years ago, Rinpoche surprised my wife and I by telling us we should go to Tibet and meet His Holiness the 17th Karmapa, and that we should go right away, that summer, and I hate to leave the house!

That trip, and a second trip that followed some years later, turned out to be pilgrimages that were also life changing. Our center in Big Rapids has a separate building as a shrine room and even a small Stupa, pictures are shown below.

I can never repay the kindness that Khenpo Rinpoche and the other rinpoches that I have taken teachings from have shown me.

The Astrology of Local Space

c 1967

Music Career

Michael Erlewine's career in music started early on, when he dropped out of high school and hitchhiked to Venice West, in Santa Monica, California, in an attempt to catch a ride on the tail end of the Beatnik era. This was 1960, and he was a little late for that, but right on time for the folk music revival that was just beginning to bloom at that time. Like many other people his age, Erlewine traveled from college center to center across the nation: Ann Arbor, Berkeley, Cambridge, and Greenwich Village. There was a well-beaten track on which traveled the young folk musicians of the future.

Erlewine, who also played folk guitar, hitchhiked for a stint with a young Bob Dylan, and then more extensively with guitar virtuoso and instrumentalist

The Astrology of Local Space

Perry Lederman. Erlewine helped to put on Dylan's first concert in Ann Arbor. He hung out with people like Ramblin' Jack Elliot, Joan Baez, The New Lost City Ramblers, and the County Gentlemen.

In 1965, the same year that the Grateful Dead were forming, Michael Erlewine, his brother Daniel, and a few others formed the first new-style band in the Midwest, the Prime Movers Blues Band. Iggy Pop was their drummer, and his stint in the band was how he got the name Iggy. This was the beginning of the hippie era. Michael was the band's lead singer, and played amplified Chicago-style blues harmonica. He still plays.

Erlewine was also the manager of the band, and personally designed and silkscreened the band's posters, one of which is shown below.

The Prime Movers became a seminal band throughout the Midwest, and even traveled as far as the West Coast, where the band spent 1967, the "summer of Love," playing at all of the famous clubs, for example, opening for Eric Clapton and Cream, at the Filmore Auditorium.

As the 60s wound down, and bands began to break up, Erlewine was still studying the music of American Blacks, in particular blues. Because of their knowledge of blues and the players, Michael and his brother Dan were invited to help host the first major electric blues festival in the United States, the 1969

The Astrology of Local Space

Ann Arbor Blues Festival. They got to wine and dine the performers, and generally look after them.

Michael interviewed (audio and video) most of the players at the first two Ann Arbor Blues Festivals, they included: Big Joe Turner, Luther Allison, Carey Bell, Bobby Bland, Clifton Chenier, James Cotton, Pee Wee Crayton, Arthur, Crudup, Jimmy Dawkins, Doctor Ross, Sleepy John Estes, Lowell Fulson, Buddy Guy, John Lee hooker, Howlin' wolf, J.B. Hutto, Albert King, B.B King, Freddie king, Sam Lay, Light-nin' Hopkins, Manse Lipscomb, Robert Lockwood, Magic Sam, Fred Mcdowell, Muddy Waters, Charlie Musslewhite, Louis Myers , Junior Parker, Brewer Phillips, Otis rush, Johnnie Shines, George Smith, Son House, Victoria Spivey, Hubert Sumlin, Sunnyland Slim, Roosevelt Sykes, Eddie Taylor, Hound Dog Taylor, Big mama Thornton, Eddie Vinson, Sippie Wallace, Junior Wells, Big Joe Williams, Robert Pete Williams, Johnny Young, and Mighty Joe Young.

Email:

Michael Erlewine can be reached at Michael@Erlewine.net

6089002R0

Made in the USA
Lexington, KY
17 July 2010